CATHOLIC BY
CHOICE

CATHOLIC BY CHOICE

Why I embraced the faith,
joined the Church, and
embarked on the adventure
of a lifetime

RICHARD COLE

LOYOLA PRESS.
A JESUIT MINISTRY
Chicago

LOYOLA PRESS.
A JESUIT MINISTRY

3441 N. Ashland Avenue
Chicago, Illinois 60657
(800) 621-1008
www.loyolapress.com

Excerpts of Robert Bly's poetry in chapter three are used by the permission of Robert Bly.

Cover art credit: ©iStockphoto.com/skodonnell
Back cover author photo, Steven Noreyko.

ISBN-13: 978-0-8294-4056-0
ISBN-10: 0-8294-4056-9
Library of Congress Control Number: 2013957226

Printed in the United States of America.
13 14 15 16 17 18 Versa 10 9 8 7 6 5 4 3 2 1

Contents

Welcome

In 1998, I went to Corpus Christi Abbey, a monastery in South Texas. The monks lived by the Rule of St. Benedict, which directs members of the community to "receive all guests like Christ." That's very much what they did. They welcomed me when I arrived and prayed for me when I left.

In 2004, due to a lack of new vocations, the monastery was closed. Some of the brothers were accepted into other communities, some of the older ones were moved to nursing facilities, and some have passed away. *Catholic by Choice* is dedicated to the spirit of that community, which continues in the church's ongoing embrace of new members, in the life that I and others have been given as Catholics, and also, to some degree I hope, in the pages that follow. Welcome.

Introduction

Let me tell you a story about Eddie. We met in a recovery program years ago, and he would tell this story about himself. Once when he was trying to stop drinking, he found himself in a psychiatric hospital. He was broke. He'd lost his job. His wife had left him. He was at the end of his last rope. Every morning, he would talk to a psychiatrist. After several sessions the doctor said, "Eddie, you're all over the map. You need to focus. I want you to go off by yourself and think about this question: What are the three things you need in order to live? The three things you absolutely have to have to keep living."

Eddie said okay, and he went off to think. A few days later, he came back with his answer.

"First of all," Eddie said, "I need to breathe." (He was taking the question seriously. He had no choice at that point.) "Second, I need to drink water. I know I can go without food for weeks. I've done it. But I need water all the time."

"Last," he said, "I need to be understood. If nobody understands me, I think I'll die."

I don't believe Eddie was being melodramatic about dying. He'd gone through too much for that. I think he was just being realistic. If we're not understood, we can die—fast or slow. It's a form of loneliness, and people all over the world die from loneliness every day. If we're not understood, we might feel simply frustrated at first, but if it continues, this frustration can rise into an ocean of despair, pain, even panic. You see this need to communicate in toddlers before they learn to talk, a compulsion that can't be explained as mere convenience. You see it in the aged and the sick. If we're not understood in some way that we truly need, it can make us older, make us ill. Our libraries are monuments of trying to be understood, with each book representing success in various degrees. This book, too, of course.

Catholic by Choice is a love story about conversion and the honeymoon of faith. It began when I visited a Benedictine monastery. I was there for only three days, to read for a while and relax. I didn't see visions or hear voices. But when I came back, I found myself on a path. I felt an invisible hand in the small of my back, gently pushing me forward. Something—I didn't know what—had happened.

What happened, in fact, was an intense, painful, and utterly dazzling two-year period during which I fell in love with God, became a Christian, and finally entered the Catholic Church. Much of the book was written a year after I joined the church, when the experience was still fresh in my mind. That was almost fifteen years ago, however, so it's natural, even appropriate, to politely ask at this point if I'm still a practicing, fully functioning Catholic. That glorious, utterly dazzling conversion that I talk so much about—did it stick?

Yes, actually, I believe it did.

After all these years, I still have my Mass "cavity," a feeling of emptiness in the center of my chest, just under the sternum, that gradually builds every week and can be filled only by going to Mass. Nothing else can fill that emptiness.

"But what about your faith?" a reader might ask. "Have you ever been faced with doubts? A dark night of the soul? And how's your family? Are the kids all right? Are you still married? Still employed? Still sober? Have you ever regretted joining the church?"

These are good questions. The Mass is the "source and summit of our Christian life," but a Catholic life is always more than showing up in the pews. Life keeps happening. We come down from the pink cloud, the honeymoon is over, and then the relatives arrive, hungry, unannounced, and asking questions at the door.

So the biggest question might be this: After recovering from the flash and enthusiasm of a manic episode that lasted literally for years, have I reached a more authentic conversion that moves beyond a peak experience to a more-balanced faith?

Probably not. I am a serial enthusiast. I keep losing my balance and falling in love, and my new life—yes, it still feels new—is very much a work in progress. But God gave me faith years ago, and he keeps giving me faith. Certainly, I have days when I forget, when I can believe something in my mind but not really in my heart. Then I recollect myself and feel a presence. God is the unexpected. It's like living next to the ocean. I don't have to look at the water to know that I'm always beside a large body, changeable but constant and scary when I think about how deep it is but calming for that very reason.

At the same time, I've been given the grace to realize how self-involved I was when I first wrote this book. Truly, I was stoned on God. I had fallen deeply in love with God, but I was also—and equally—in love with the pretty idea of myself in love with God. I wanted a life of spiritual beauty, as if I were making a work of art. Fortunately, that phase didn't last forever. These days I try to talk less and listen more.

Meanwhile, God is patient. My conversion put such a strain on my wife and kids that I'm still grateful that they didn't walk out on me.

They stayed, though, and everyone is in good shape. The boys are now twenty-two and eighteen. Harrison is in college, and Spencer is finishing his last year of homeschooling. They haven't settled on any careers yet, and that's fine with their parents. As Lauren says, what they wind up doing for a living probably hasn't even been invented yet.

As for my business career, such as it is, I quit the job I talked about in the book, moved to my fourth hi-tech startup (a triumph of faith over reason), and finally got laid off when the dot-com bubble collapsed. I now have a modest business as a freelance writer, and Lauren works with me as chief financial officer, editor, and proofreader.

There have been bumps along the way. A few years ago I decided I could start drinking again. Big mistake. I figured that I could just drink wine, a bit of bourbon, have a civilized little party as a sensible adult. But certain guests—such as anger, anxiety, exhaustion, and two kinds of depression—kept showing up. I didn't invite you guys, I said, and they all said, the hell you didn't. So I went back and forth, dithering as some of us do, gradually drinking more and slipping back to where I was twenty years before. I realized that I wasn't the empty vessel for God that Scripture talks about, if only because my own little vessel was always filled with a drink. So I finally asked God one morning in prayer, Do you want me to stop drinking? And God said yes. Period. He didn't say it twice. So now I'm back to working my program, and this time, I sincerely pray, it's for good.

Lauren and I have also had our bumps. We're still not on the same page when it comes to the church, but our pages overlap. She's still a model of faith for me, and I see her serving others far more than I do.

Catholicism has legs. That's what I try to explain to Catholic initiates these days. I want to reassure them that the road they see in front of them never stops. If my own experience is any measure, they'll never reach a point where there's nothing left to say or read or do. I once heard someone assert that he had "read himself out of the church," but I know that you can also read yourself back in, and the longer I read, the more I'm amazed at what is still in front of me: teachings, saints, forms of prayers, history, and traditions going back for centuries. I tell those initiates it's like finding an interesting pebble, something small and local, then looking up to see that you're on a small mound, then looking again to find that you're actually at the foot of a mountain that's backed by even higher mountains, and then, faint in the distance, the Himalayas with something even larger beyond.

There's a catch, though. Although the Catholic Church is a big table, we have to find our own unique place at the table, the one that belongs to us and to no one else. To me, this means finding the parish where I can grow as a Christian and best serve others in specific ministries. We also need to remember that our proper place at the table might change from time to time. Father Thomas Keating once said that "the god of your childhood doesn't exist," and I would suggest that the church of our childhood doesn't exist either. We have to believe as adults, and that means living that belief at the table, in community with others. A faith formed in solitude is not what this church is about. You can't be a Catholic on a desert island.

So we all gather at Mass, the heart of the church and the body of Christ, but to keep this body alive, the heart has to keep beating. We can stop this heart if we choose. It's within our power. We're the living blood of this heart, and a heart stops beating if the blood stops flowing in from the veins. The church needs attendance, new members, new ideas, and a renewal of vows from all of us. But a heart also stops beating if the arteries harden and can't carry the blood away. If we stay huddled inside our Catholic world, the church runs the danger of becoming rigid, stagnant, and eventually lifeless. So we need to gather with God and one another at Mass, and then, filled with the bright oxygen of the Holy Spirit, we need to leave, to go outside and share the Good News with the world.

However, the world's reaction to us can be a challenge. The church is a lightning rod these days for all sorts of issues, from gender and sexuality to the whole idea of hierarchy, so if you're leading the Catholic life and you find yourself becoming a lightning rod, it helps to be well grounded. For me, grounded means community, study, and prayer—and all three centered on Christ. Is it worth all that effort? Absolutely. And I'll tell you another thing: if you keep moving forward in your faith, your life will never, ever, *ever* be boring.

So please, take my hand. Let me tell you a story. In the middle of my life, in the middle of a desert I could barely see, I discovered a vein of silver in the side of a mountain, an amazing, almost unbelievable treasure that everyone can share. I found that Someone is here, and I don't mean an impersonal "force." I mean Someone who loves us and knows us better than we'll ever know ourselves. We are not alone. We are understood.

1

Corpus Christi Abbey

Wednesday

I'm singing in a monastery. A real monastery with real monks dressed in black habits. This is my first day of a three-day visit. We're singing prayers at Vespers, five o'clock in the afternoon.

The singing stops. We sit in silence.

Why am I here? To get a bit of rest. Read a few books. That's what I thought, anyway. Now, I'm not sure.

If I had any religious motives for taking this trip, I'd probably be the last one to know. I've kept a journal since I was twelve, but I'm still my own biggest blind spot. Some days I look in the mirror and just see skin. Am I pretending to be spiritual, a monk-for-a-day? I don't have the right to call myself religious. I don't worship. Don't even pray, to speak of. But here I am.

So what am I looking for? I've already gone down the buffet line—Zen, living for art, heavy drinking, recovery, t'ai chi, New Age, witchcraft—looking for what? Truth? A piece of quartz? All I want is a philosophy I can live with.

"All?" The word rolls around in my head and fades into a slight question. It's so damn quiet in this place, you start to hear things. I think of all the churches I've known. The Methodist church I was dragged to as a boy, which I left as soon as I could. The fundamentalist

1

churches that still scare me. I think of the mild Quakers I knew in Brooklyn and their meetings that I attended for a few months as a "sojourner." I almost, almost joined, but I lost my nerve at the last minute and left.

I look around the church as we sing. I was expecting the Hollywood version of a monastery, something European looking, with vineyards and massive stone buildings and ivy-covered cloisters. I wanted sturdy monks singing with deep, vibrant voices, like the Gregorian chant CDs that I play at home when I take a hot bath and light candles and sticks of incense.

When I got here this afternoon, I saw nothing that was even remotely European. The main building looks like a cheap motel, with tacky brick veneer and a flat, gravel-and-tar roof. The sidewalks need sweeping; the brush needs cutting back. We're surrounded by chaparral over six feet high. Nature is moving in.

The church is tidy and very clean, but it's made of plastic Quonset huts. (Where do they get Quonset huts these days? Army surplus?) The Quonsets have been cut lengthwise and placed side by side, with a third on top in the middle, forming a single, large interior space. Everything looks a bit provisional, though the abbey has been here for more than twenty years.

Now we're singing again. Our voices are not exactly deep and sonorous either. We struggle with a scrawny little string of melody that just barely floats over the notes from the little organ.

"Fear . . . of the Lord . . . is the beginning of wisdom," we sing, barely. Almost every man in the stalls seems to be at least in his sixties. Some must be in their eighties. I saw the older ones arriving at the church doors in golf carts. They got out slowly and walked with canes.

We finish up, our chants fading under the roar of the rattling air conditioners. *Pitiful.* The word bubbles up, and I gently push it away.

I'm not Catholic. I'm not Christian. Do I even believe in God? I tell people that I pray, I just don't know who I'm talking to. I thought that was witty.

At the end of the service, an older monk struggles to get up to leave. One of the younger guys, only about sixty or so, has been sitting next to him with a sour look on his face. But as the old monk rises, the younger one looks up and a smile suddenly fills his face, as if he'd just noticed that his father was sitting next to him. He helps the old man put on his baseball cap, takes him by the arm, and opens the back door.

As the two monks maneuver their way outside, I can see through the open door, above the Quonset huts, a little square of empty sky, a pale blue. It's already twilight, later than I thought. Then the door shuts like a vault and almost immediately the air conditioner stops. A broad silence fills the room. The other monks don't budge, and we continue to sit. Maybe we're supposed to be praying now or meditating; I don't know. I think of that glimpse of sky, how pretty it looked, how calm.

⚜

My wife gave me this trip as a present for my forty-ninth birthday. A few months ago, she had seen a small ad in the back of *Texas Monthly* magazine for the Benedictine Retreat Center at Corpus Christi Abbey in Sandia, Texas. I had a certificate for a three-day stay, Wednesday to Friday.

When she gave the gift, I immediately wanted to say no. "I can't go to a *monastery*," I told her. "They'll card me at the door." But the idea sank in. I'd be visiting during the week, so I'd be the only guest. I could attend prayers. I could eat meals with the brothers. It would be just me and the monks, a small, select circle. The elite. The thought was appealing.

The night before I left, Lauren and I bundled our boys in blankets, and we all went out to the backyard to watch the Leonid meteor shower. We lay on our backs in the middle of the yard, staring up into the darkness. Every few minutes a tiny streak of light zipped across the sky and winked out. I didn't believe in omens, but, of course, I looked for them. After a while, the boys fell asleep, and Lauren and I carried them inside.

The next morning I packed a small bag, grabbed some books, said good-bye to everybody, and headed south.

I wasn't driving far, only from Austin to a point north of Corpus Christi, a bit under two hundred miles, but the trip took over eight hours because I followed the directions from the monastery. The map they mailed me was oddly complicated, ignoring the interstate highways and leading me along an older network of country roads, each one smaller than the last. That's fine, I thought. Like most Americans, I rush for a living, and by then I was tired of rushing. I left the main highway outside Austin and started down farm-to-market roads, poking along in my little Subaru, my burro.

As I drove, I felt pleasantly self-conscious about being on a "pilgrimage." For the past few days I'd been reading about monasteries. I even read a bit of the Bible. I wanted to be prepped for any Significant Moments, any experiences that might cost-justify my work as a seeker.

Pilgrim or no pilgrim, I was also very aware that I was fast approaching fifty and my life was changing. The year before, I had suddenly lost a lot of weight, and my vision became blurry. I went to the doctor and was diagnosed as diabetic. It could have been worse, of course, but I was rattled. I had always been smug about being one of the chronically healthy. But now I had a disease without a cure and all sorts of complications if I didn't take care of myself. I felt fine. Was

I sick? I guess so. But I knew for sure that I was no longer twenty-five and immortal, or forty-five and invincible. I was forty-nine and probable.

The sun rose, the hours passed, the small towns grew smaller. I drove though crossroad hamlets with a feed store, a 99-cent discount center, a Dairy Queen, a barbecue restaurant or two, and rows of pickups parked along the main street with a yellow blinker at the intersection. I saw a beauty salon with a sign in front: "Come in and Tell Laverne Happy Birthday." I passed small, white, wooden churches—"Full Power Gospel"—announcing Judgment Day and the glory of Jesus Christ.

By the middle of the afternoon, I reached the Gulf Coastal Plain. The flat Texas landscape flattened out even more, billiard-table flat, and the sky seemed bigger than before. Farmland was replaced by mesquite and cactus. We were in ranch country now. I moved along at fifty, then forty miles an hour. Time seemed to be slowing down. I tapped the gas gauge; it didn't seem to be moving. I felt as if I'd been driving for days. I thought of "The Rime of the Ancient Mariner" when the sailing ship was becalmed in the tropics—"as idle as a painted ship upon a painted ocean"—but that was okay. I was in no hurry.

I crossed Interstate 37—civilization!—and then plunged back into the wilderness. I felt I was moving farther and farther away from cities, traffic, televisions, newspapers, and noise, from just about everything. I could see a few ranch houses and trailers, but I was the only car on the road. I began to notice big raptors—hawks, falcons, and large, beautifully exotic black and white birds that I later learned were caracaras. These meat eaters weren't city birds. They were completely *not* intimidated by humans. In fact, they sat just a few feet from the shoulder of the road with a "So what do *you* want?" look on their face, staring straight at me as I drove past.

Around 4:00 in the afternoon, I turned off the last highway and promptly got lost. Like a fairy tale, I thought—first, you have to lose your way. After some back-and-forthing, I found the right turn, drove down a dirt road, then another one. I came to a fork in the road with a large wooden cross. A weathered sign said Peace. I could see some buildings just beyond, on a bluff overlooking Lake Corpus Christi.

I stopped at the main building. Inside the front door, a monk was sitting at a little desk, listening to *A Prairie Home Companion* on the radio. He was wearing a black habit. Neat, I thought. At least they still wear habits. On the phone he called the guest master. After a few minutes, Brother James came out, a short, stocky man with a barrel chest and a broad, confident smile. He walked me over to the Quonset huts that served as dormitories. Each dormitory is a hut named after a Benedictine saint: St. Bede, St. Scholastica. I was given a room in St. Meinrad Hall. Brother James gave me a schedule, wished me success, then disappeared.

So here I am, on my own. My room is narrow but tidy. A single bed. Shower. Closet. The schedule is basically the same every day: Lauds at 7:00. Mass at 7:30. Noon prayers at 11:30. Evening prayers at 5:00. I look at a sign on the wall:

> We pray that you will experience a prayerful, peaceful stay here, and that you return. Please maintain an atmosphere conducive to prayer and reflection by speaking softly at all times. THANK YOU FOR YOUR COOPERATION! GOD BLESS YOU!

I have three days.

Thursday

I get up at 5:00 a.m. Monk for a day. Actually, I want to make a cup of coffee in the kitchenette that's open all night. I get dressed and step outside. A wet, heavy fog has moved in during the night, coastal damp, and everything is covered with dew. In the kitchenette, I clear away the dead bugs from the sink and try the faucet. The pipes shudder, and rusty water spurts out, turning clear after a few moments. Good enough. I make instant coffee and sit reading at the card table.

At seven, I walk up the hill toward the Quonset church. At the top, a life-size statue of Jesus emerges from the fog. His arms are raised. On his chest I see a burning heart tied with a ribbon, radiating beams of light. His expression is mild, attentive.

Lauds was like Vespers last night. Again we chant our way through the service, flying on just one engine, wavering and sputtering, but we finally make it home. Prayers are followed by Mass. The entire monastery community is in attendance: about a dozen brothers and a priest. A few people from the neighborhood show up, local ranchers it looks like, and some older couples. One woman sits in the middle pew, very focused. She's maybe in her early sixties, though it's hard to tell, with short, gray hair that's neatly cut. She sits up straight, looking very no-nonsense.

I follow the Mass as best I can. Stand, cross yourself, sit, kneel, stand, kneel. Cross-cross-cross. Everybody seems to know the drill.

After breakfast I walk around the grounds. The monastery is on one of the high points on this side of Lake Corpus Christi. The lake is big—three miles across and ten miles long. On the far horizon I see tiny trucks crawling along the interstate. I walk down to the pier. I find a wooden tackle box labeled "For Monks Only," but the lid is broken and it's empty. The railings need repair, and the pier is sagging on one side. I get the impression that this monastery has seen more active days. Now they have only a few visitors, like me. The monks are kind but seem tired and ineffective. I even wonder if these communities attract the best and the brightest. Or maybe I'm using standards that don't belong here. *Dear schlumps of God.* I should write that down.

On my way back from the lake, I discover a path that disappears into the chaparral. I follow it for a dozen yards and discover a grotto for Our Lady of Guadalupe. It's small and humble, made out of cinderblocks. Inside, there's a painting of Our Lady, encased in a wooden frame painted red and white, and sealed in glass. Someone has taken a shot at the painting. They missed Our Lady but hit the glass. A web of fractures radiates from the bullet hole. A small bouquet has been placed in the hole. Petals hang over the sharp edge of the glass, brown and wilted.

I've brought only a few books with me: a Bible, *The Goddess of the Americas*, which my wife gave me about Our Lady of Guadalupe, and a collection of essays by Simone Weil. I've been reading Weil for the past few weeks, and I admire her enormously. She never joined the church for various reasons, but she remained waiting faithfully at the threshold all her life. I think I can understand that sort of devotion, as well as her reservation. Something about waiting at the threshold seems humble and honest to me. I read a passage Weil wrote about baptism:

> It may . . . be that my life will come to an end before I have ever felt this impulse. But one thing is absolutely certain. It is that if one day it comes about that I love God enough to deserve the grace of baptism, I shall receive this grace on that very day. . . . In that case why should I have any anxiety? It is not my business to think about myself. My business is to think about God. It is for God to think about me.

Elsewhere she says, "Faith without understanding, necessarily." What does she mean by that?

Somewhere else: "Expect nothing."

Before evening prayers, I write in my notebook, "A dawn inside me. But how to break open the dawn?" I look at the words. Who am I trying to impress? Who's looking over my shoulder as I write?

At supper, Brother James asks, "Did you have a successful day?" I like the word *successful*, though I can't think of a reply. So far, nothing "dramatic" has happened. I'm starting to wonder whether I'm getting my money's worth, so to speak. I've heard that the abbey has a spiritual director, Carmen, who lives nearby. They call her a hermit. What does that mean? I think of some grizzled old woman in a trailer, living on dry bread and grasshoppers. I make an appointment to talk to her on Saturday, the last thing I'll do before I leave.

Back at my room, I look at Weil again: "God waits like a beggar who stands motionless and silent before someone who might perhaps give him a piece of bread." I'm dubious. I think of the beggars I knew in New York, the usual panhandlers, some of them crackheads, holding out their hands. I also think of a Buddhist monk I used to see in Chinatown. He would always be walking very slowly and deliberately, heel to toe, through the crowds, holding a wooden bowl for alms. He looked straight ahead, and it seemed that he was always seething with anger, infuriated at having to beg but doing it anyway because he was a proper monk. I thought about him a lot, but I never had the courage to talk to him. I never learned his story, and I never gave him money.

I turn off the lights. It's stuffy. I turn on the lights, start the air conditioner, turn off the lights, and get back into bed. The air conditioner rattles. I can sleep through roars but not rattles. I get up, turn it off and get into bed again. As I lie in the darkness, I remember a poem by

Charles Wright about wanting to be pierced by God. Hey, I'd like to be pierced by God too, assuming I knew it was God doing the piercing. I'd like to be like Christ—who wouldn't?—though without the Crucifixion, of course. I'd like to find spiritual wisdom, but I'm not sure I want to sacrifice anything major. Do you have to die for wisdom? Maybe that's old fashioned.

Pray for the truth, whatever that is.

Friday

At lunch, I start to serve myself, but Brother James catches me with a smile. We all join hands in a circle and say grace. We sit down to fish and steamed vegetables with mashed potatoes, and no dessert. The meal looks a bit discouraged, very simple and low-cost, like cafeteria meals at a country school.

I sit at the visitors table with James. The other monks sit at their own table. One sits at the very end by himself, against the wall with a "Don't Talk to Me" expression. I guess your privacy is well respected here. A woman in her thirties comes in late, gets her meal, and sits down with us. I saw her earlier that morning in a field next to the abbey, wrestling hay bales off the back of her pickup. A strong country woman. She crosses herself, says a silent prayer, crosses herself again, and starts eating. I'm happy to be in a place where you can be totally unselfconscious about your faith.

A young monk I haven't seen before, maybe around twenty, moves his tray over to our table and sits down next to her. "Is this a private party or can anyone join?" he asks with a smile. I wonder if he's flirting. They talk about religion. She says that she's Catholic now but grew up fundamentalist Christian. "Hardshell," she says. "Preachers'd be yellin' at us, even little children. Little children would be crying right there in the middle of church. I couldn't take that."

"Would you consider Judaism?" he asks.

"Nope. I'm not Jewish."

"Islam?"

"Nope. Too extreme. Catholic's the way for me." She takes a big helping of mashed potatoes, and they move on to other topics.

Odd to say, but I've never thought of Catholicism as something you actually joined. I grew up as a middle-class white kid in small-town Texas, and I was taught that Catholicism was basically a Mexican thing. Catholics were brown; they were born that way. Studying to become a Catholic would be like training to be Chinese. In my extended family, "church" meant a Protestant church, usually Methodist. If you were really gung-ho about your religion (something my parents considered to be a bit, well, lower class), you joined one of the charismatic or Bible churches. The idea that this woman actually joined the Catholic Church is a curious idea. Intriguing.

In the afternoon I take another walk down to the lake. I still have the feeling that I should be doing something, making some effort some-how. I walk over to the grotto of Our Lady of Guadalupe. I pause. Okay, I'll take the plunge. I kneel in the gravel, put my hands together, close my eyes. *What in God's name am I doing?* I think about that bullet hole. It would be an easy shot from the lake. I keep kneeling, though.

The word *incrimination* pops up in my head, and voices are saying, "You've incriminated yourself. You were spotted at the scene of the crime. We have witnesses. The monks said you were praying." Christ broke the law, and look what happened to him.

I get up, knees sore from the gravel, and study the bullet hole in the glass. Does somebody around here have a beef with Catholics? With religion? Or was it just vandalism and tomfoolery?

At Vespers that evening, I find myself saying, "Lord God have mercy on us, Lord God have mercy on us," over and over as the monks chant along. I want to pray. I really do. I keep cranking the engine, but nothing starts.

Saturday

I wake up every hour through the night. What am I doing here? Am I wasting my time? Have I been productive?

I get up before dawn to make coffee in the kitchenette and read. Around six, a brother in his habit comes in, the younger one who was talking to the lady guest at lunch. I know there's some sort of regulation about eating or drinking before Mass. He gets a Coke from the vending machine, gives me a quick, guilty smile, and disappears into the dark.

After prayers, Mass, and breakfast, I pack the car and go to the retreat office to meet with Carmen. I'm early and wait outside on the sidewalk. I start to worry that she might not show up, but at 9:00 on the dot she appears as if out of nowhere and says hello. This is the no-nonsense woman I saw at Mass. She has an accent that I can't place. Not Mexican. Maybe Spanish. We go to one of the Quonset huts and sit down in what looks like a consulting room. Just us, two chairs, and a little desk.

I've been thinking about what I should ask. I want to sound intelligent and halfway literate when it comes to the Bible, so I ask her about the concept of poverty of spirit. What does it mean, exactly, when Christ said, "Blessed are the poor in spirit"?

She shakes the question away—no nonsense—and looks at me directly. "Who is God to you? Do you pray? Who do you pray to?"

I flounder. "Well, uh, yes, I do pray . . . Sort of."

"And who is God to you?"

I was hoping she wouldn't ask. "God is, hmm, well, like a swirling galaxy. A large force. Something big. Powerful. Something like a river, maybe."

She places her fingertips together. "When you pray, what word do you use?"

"I've been saying 'Lord' the past few days. Sometimes 'Jesus'."

"And you don't feel odd, addressing him as Lord?"

No, I tell her. Maybe I'm lying because I want to say the right thing. She's intense. I tell her that I feel odd being here at the monastery, out of place, but for some reason I don't feel odd using those words.

We talk for an hour, me listening mostly. I desperately want to take notes, but don't, trying as hard as I can to remember what she's saying. Somehow, everything suddenly seems significant.

She says, "God is mysterious. We can't understand what he's doing many times, but remember that he is always leading you to himself. Sometimes fast. Sometimes more slowly. But always, always, he's leading you."

And she says, "You are being created, very deliberately, at God's own pace. It's like being pregnant, or cooking. If the soup takes three hours to make, you can't rush it. Just wait. And while you're waiting, you have to trust. You can't presume to know what God is doing. That's not faith; it's a false security. You simply have to have faith."

"I've always looked for a system," I tell her, "but at the same time I've always been reluctant to really adopt a system."

"Christianity isn't a system," she says. "It's a Person. The Person of Jesus Christ. Everything else—doctrine, dogma, church membership—just revolves around this person."

I tell her that I was worried that I hadn't accomplished much over this retreat, that maybe I was wasting my time.

"Don't worry about that," she says. "You can't pray your way to heaven. You can't control the process. You might even go on a detour. But God will always draw you back, helping you along."

She leans forward. "Remember, you are a work of art by God. You are a masterpiece! You've already taken the first steps. [I have?!!] God is helping you every step of the way. Your path is exactly as it should be, at the pace it should be. God wants you to find him. Your understanding might occur in a splendid, wonderful moment. That sometimes happens. Or it might develop very slowly over time. But whatever occurs is God's handiwork, and his work is perfect and right on schedule."

The hour is up. I realize that I've never had a conversation like this before in my life. It's one thing to talk and read about religion and spirituality, but this is different. I feel as if this conversation were happening to someone else. Carmen wasn't testing or trying to convert me or asking if I'd been saved. She was simply talking to me as if I were already on a spiritual path, all very matter of fact, like the monks.

Uncertain and grateful, I thank her for her time. "It's my job," she says and shows me the door.

I walk slowly back to the main building to hand in my room key and check out. The brother at the front desk is reading a little pamphlet.

"I enjoyed my stay," I tell him, handing him a check.

"Good," he says, nodding. Pause.

Fishing for something more, I say, "Perhaps I'll be back."

"Good," he says, smiling slightly.

Pause. "Well, thanks for everything."

Then he says, "God bless you." A soft ping inside. That's it. To be blessed, and especially blessed by a real monk. I feel like I've gotten my money's worth. I thank him and leave.

⟡

I drive back the way I came and get lost again. This time I wind up at a Baptist lakeside retreat. It looks a lot fancier than the abbey. Then I find the highway and head north. I keep asking myself, *What's happened? Anything? Am I the same? Different? What's the story*

I take the fast way back, following the interstate. Along the way I keep thinking about what I might say when I walk in the door. I've been to a monastery—such as it is—but it's a real one. I see myself walk in quietly. Lauren looks up, smiling, and starts to say hello. Then she looks at my face and hesitates. At that very moment, she instinctively realizes that something has indeed happened. There's an expression, a light in my eyes, something she hasn't seen before. I'll greet her with a humble peace that radiates from my every pore. Even the boys will feel it. They'll come tumbling into the room and pause, then slowly approach me like doves drawn to St. Francis. I'll gather my family in my arms, and we'll sit for a moment, happy in the quiet I've brought with me from the abbey.

I walk in the door. Lauren's on the telephone with the air conditioning repairman. She waves and keeps talking about how the compressor is making this *errrrrrrrrrrgh* grinding sound, like it's working too hard. The boys wander in, and we hug, and I tell them that I have some really cool bird feathers I found at the monastery. Hey, wow, they say, and go back to their TV show.

Lauren gets off the phone and gives me a hug. "So how was it?"

Spencer, our four-year-old, runs into the kitchen, crying that his brother called him a poopy head, and Harrison yells from the front TV room that he didn't. Then Harrison follows Spencer into the kitchen, and they start arguing. Over the squabble I shout, "I think . . . I'm beginning—just beginning, mind you—to think about a personal God."

We separate the boys, get them settled again, and go back to the kitchen. I show Lauren the feathers, and I tell her a bit about the monastery. She listens to me carefully. She's my best friend in the world and knows me better than anyone. She's also a cradle Catholic, though she hasn't been to Mass for years. I wind down after a bit, and then she asks, "You go to Mass there?"

"Sure. Every day with the monks in the morning."

"Ah."

If I had been more astute, less wrapped up in myself, I would have seen that little "ah" as significant. But I bat it away.

"You going to church this Sunday?" she asks, giving me a wifely look.

"I guess so," I say casually, but suddenly I'm thinking about going to Mass, and I feel a deep flurry of happiness. The feeling is intense and reassuring precisely because it is so intense. I'm sitting calmly at the kitchen table, but inside I'm a wild man and shouting, "Of course I'm going to Mass! Are you crazy?! Of course I'm going! Of course!"

2

My Catholic Passport

More than anything else, the monks gave me permission. By accepting me into their community for a few days, letting me warm myself by the fire, they gave me the confidence to walk into any Catholic church in the world and attend Mass. This was amazing to me. I felt that going to Mass was the most incredible privilege I'd ever been given in my life. Now if somebody carded me at the door, I had a ticket, a passport, stamped and monk-approved. I'd been to a real monastery. If I was good enough for the monks, I was good enough for any parish on earth. No matter that I wasn't a believer. I didn't know what I believed. And I accepted the fact that I couldn't take communion. I only knew that I was unbelievably happy to be in a Catholic church.

I started going to Mass every Sunday. It was the high point of my week, and I thought about it all week long. Then Lauren told me that I could go to Mass every day if I wanted. I shook my head, unable to believe my incredible good fortune. Mass every single day! Even Baptists only have Sunday and Wednesday prayer meetings.

I looked at an Austin map and found a regular noontime Mass at the chapel at St. Edward's University in south Austin. I started taking long lunch hours and went once during the week, then twice, then three times a week. My job could wait.

Mass at St. Edward's was an oasis of calm in the middle of the business day, and as the months went by, it became an important part of my Catholic life. The chapel was a small wooden building painted white. Somewhere I read that it was originally a pistol range. The floors were carpeted, a bit spongy as you walked down the aisle to take a seat. Attendance was small, usually just me, some Holy Cross brothers, nuns, maybe a student or two, but that gave the services a sweet, intimate feel. And Father Rick's homilies were exactly what I needed: brief and well-considered, a portable bit of wisdom I could remember easily and carry through the rest of the day.

I also got on the Web and checked out the schedules and locations of other Catholic churches around Austin. I could go to the dawn patrol at 6:30 at the cathedral downtown, or to a dozen different Masses at noon or at 5:00, 5:20, 5:30, or 5:45. I could even go at night sometimes. Catholics made it easy. Nobody ever asked me for ID, and on top of everything else, Mass was free!

Was I going through a conversion? I didn't know. I didn't care. I just wanted to go to Mass. It made me feel calm and good inside, a feeling I'd never known before. I was so focused on the Mass that it took me a couple of weeks before I finally and very reluctantly admitted, *This Catholic thing probably has something to do with God . . .* And then it took a week after that before I also admitted that, yes, *sigh*, being Catholic probably meant being Christian as well. Not Protestant Christian but still Christian. I didn't even like the sound of the word *Christian*. I thought of TV evangelists with their pompadours and polyester suits, screeching, "Jaysus! Jaysus!" from a plywood pulpit. Jaysus was going to be a problem. Jaysus had a reputation. He didn't leave you alone; he had issues. But I'd deal with that later. Right then, I just wanted to go to Mass.

I began to learn the liturgy. Some parts always seemed to be the same. I read that Mass was like going up and down two mountains.

You marched up the first mountain, the Liturgy of the Word, praying for forgiveness and praising God, then down the other side, listening to a reading from the Old Testament usually, or sometimes the New Testament, then a psalm, then the Gospel and the sermon (or homily, as those Catholics called it). Then you marched up the next mountain, the Liturgy of the Eucharist, to give an offering. Then the Host was raised, and the Catholics got to receive communion.

So far, so good. But just as I thought I had the hang of it, the priest would slip in a new prayer I'd never heard before or do some new routine. And sometimes the Host would be distributed but not consecrated by a priest. What was that all about? I needed a script.

Still, I loved the ritual, even though it felt slightly unreal when I attended, as though I were a character in a movie. I would enter the cool darkness of the church and feel myself slowly splitting into two persons. One part of me crossed himself with holy water and knelt and prayed. The other part of me would watch all this, shaking his head, asking, "Uh, Richard, just exactly what do you think you're doing?"

Maybe I was playing a role. I could feel my Protestant ancestors perking up, scrutinizing me. But I also knew that if I was just playing a role, the hunger to play it was absolutely real and growing stronger every day.

The weeks went by, and the Catholic thing kept snowballing. I don't want to exaggerate, but I honestly thought my heart was going to explode. Whether this was a new toy or a new vision, I knew I had something beautiful in my life, a nourishment that was gradually seeping into my heart, and the more I received, the more I wanted, and I realized how parched and desperate I'd been. I was overwhelmed by gratitude. I wasn't thinking about becoming a Catholic. I didn't want to join anything. Just being there in church—a real, live Catholic church!—was enough. I think if someone had told me that, sorry, I could never join, I could never take communion, that would have been fine. I would have been content to just stay in the pews, as long as I could come in from the cold and attend Mass.

I began waking up every morning before dawn. My eyes would snap open, I'd make some coffee, start to read, and try to pray. I got up at 5:30, then 5:00, then 4:30 every morning, seven days a week. (Like a monk!) There were never enough hours to read.

I decided to read the whole Bible, cover to cover, even if it took me a year. And I made a promise to read every word out loud. I didn't want to skip over anything, and I didn't want the reading to be just mental. I wanted it to be an action, not just a thought, with each word coming physically out of my throat.

I was an explorer standing on a mountaintop, like Balboa, gazing for the first time at a huge ocean I never even knew existed. I was a little boy in a candy store. I was five years old, ready to bust I was so excited. I was a student again, starting fresh with a clean notebook and textbooks that smelled like new ink and made a fresh, cracking sound when you opened them for the first time.

A psychologist might argue that my Catholicism was simply a coping mechanism, a way to deal with a normal midlife crisis. Some men buy a red sports car; I was going to Mass. Religion is an obvious compensation for a personal lack in other areas. "God" simply fills a gap in your life. But you can turn that around and say that God doesn't fill gaps in our lives. He creates a world with gaps, and through these gaps we're given the grace to fall into his arms.

So yes, I was falling in love, the deep kind that happens maybe once or twice in a lifetime. I knew it was love because I'd gone through the same feelings with Lauren. When we were first together, I was completely confused. I stammered a lot. I couldn't focus. "Who *is* this person?" Too many feelings were spinning around. I only knew that I was wildly attracted to her physically, to all those outward and visible signs. After we more or less moved in together, I remember how every morning she would kiss me before she left for work. I would still be half asleep, and her perfume smelled like apples, pleasing and unexpected.

I felt the same dizziness when I entered church. I loved how the woodwork and the walls gave off the faint smell of incense. I loved crossing myself at the door and feeling the holy water, with maybe a little drop trickling down my forehead as I walked down the aisle. I loved kneeling on those kneeler things on the back of the pew and crossing myself and standing and sitting. I loved the whole gloriously complicated beauty of the Mass. Catholics knew that God was beautiful, and with all their rituals and habits and the weird statues and icons and secret symbols and devotional cards and rosaries and warm banks of candles flickering in front of Our Lady, they were simply acknowledging and celebrating this beauty. *Richness* was a word I kept using. Catholics were like these spiritual trust-fund babies, unbelievably rich with a two-thousand-year-old religious culture stacked on another three thousand years of Hebraic culture. Old World richness, European and Middle Eastern. Best of all, I could share this richness, even if I couldn't actually eat at the table. I could watch, and nobody would tell me to leave. I had my ticket.

I knew it was love because I was scared. Again, it was the same kind of fear I felt when I'd first met Lauren, the realization that my life was changing whether I wanted it to change or not. I went back to a journal I had kept then:

> I have no control anymore over what's happening. I see myself riding on the back of a panther through the jungle, then we're racing along the edge of a cliff. On one side this dark, dangerous tangle, on the other a drop into empty space. There's no way I can get off.

Part of me was panicked about losing control over who I was, or thought I was. At the same time, I worried that this wonderful, scary feeling might go away. Like a fairy tale, the enchantment would be broken, the spell reversed. I even worried that someday I might be turned away from the church, that I couldn't attend Mass. During the week, when I went to noon Mass at St. Ed's, I was always nervous as I walked up to the chapel. The front door has a plain brass doorknob. As in a dream, I saw my hand reaching out to turn the knob, and every time, I was afraid that it would be locked. Every time the knob turned in my hand and the door swung open, but it took months before that fear went away.

I also felt that this was True Love because it hurt. I mean literally, like a sore muscle. My heart hurt in my chest, and it only got worse. In the mornings when I was reading the Bible in the kitchen, chanting along, I'd sometimes pause and then start crying. I don't know why. I would suddenly have the feeling of possibility, of loving and being loved in a way I'd never experienced, even in marriage. I felt that I wasn't alone, would never be alone anymore, that God or Jesus or somebody or something was sitting right there at the kitchen table with me, and I kept on crying and sometimes wound up on the sofa or under the table, sobbing like my heart would break. I hadn't cried, really cried, like that for years. This was radical, and it went on for days and weeks and months, as if I were playing catch-up after a lifetime of being a good soldier, my jaw clenched.

I remember at the time watching a heart operation on TV. The surgeons took a saw, like a circular saw, and chewed straight down the patient's chest, cracking open the sternum. Then they took an instrument that looked like a vise, only with the faces turned outwards, inserted it, and then went crank-crank-crank, and you saw the whole rib cage spreading apart—it was unnerving to watch—until there was the heart, this big wet muscle flopping around. It looked ready to jump out almost any second. I watched the operation, thinking, *That's me*, as if God were performing long-overdue surgery.

The kitchen crying finally got to the point where I asked Jesus, "Can we slow down a bit? Do I have to go through this every single morning? My heart hurts. My stomach muscles hurt. Can we take a little break?"

And that's what happened. The crying stopped, or at least slowed down. Of course, then I worried that maybe I'd prayed for the wrong thing.

You have to understand how strange, even bizarre, this religious stuff was for somebody like me. It was even stranger because I came from a Protestant background. One of my uncles is a Methodist minister. My sister is very tight with her Methodist church. My parents were married in the Methodist church, and I was baptized a Methodist. Throughout my family, back through the generations, there's not a single Catholic, not for probably five centuries. There was something taboo, even spooky about the Catholics. Who knew what went on behind those walls? I would sometimes step inside one of their churches, always with the small fear that I would do something wrong and a priest or nun would suddenly fly out of the shadows with glaring eyes and rap my knuckles with a ruler.

That was fascinating to think about, actually, and now here I was, in this forbidden zone, and the fascination was overwhelming. I have a friend who once went to live in Guatemala. When she came back to the States, she said she had fallen in love with the country. "What did you love about it?" I asked.

"Everything," she said. "I loved the jungles, the cities, the little towns up in the mountains. I loved the language. I loved the people, how they looked and talked and dressed. I loved the smells from the marketplaces, and how the women made tortillas and cooked them over charcoal fires. I loved the festivals. I loved the buses. I loved absolutely everything about that country."

Catholicism was my own Guatemala, my exotic country, and along with everything else, I loved it because it was foreign to me. It was somewhere I could start fresh, without having to untangle my feelings about the churches I'd known in the past. I could check my Protestant baggage at the door.

As I went to Mass and slowly began to understand the liturgy, every word and gesture resonated more and more. I stared at the Host as the priest took it in both hands and raised it to heaven. That little wafer now seemed like a diamond chip, a point of intersection, a crux between the visible and invisible universe, and as he raised it in consecration and the little bell rang, it seemed that two supertankers were crashing together in a single, glorious moment. I was dazzled—and grateful that I was dazzled.

Lauren watched me carefully as I stumbled and danced through these changes. She seemed distant, but maybe I made that assumption because she wasn't in the constant state of high froth that I was. Still, she taught me how to cross myself: forehead, heart, left, then right. "Feels pretty natural, doesn't it?" she asked me, and yes, I said, it did.

She was glad for me, but she also told me—I'd heard these stories before—how painful it had been for her to go to church with her father when she was a child. Her mother would always stay home. Mom wasn't Catholic; she usually had a younger child to care for, and besides, she didn't like going to church, period. Lauren's father had grown up in a severely observant, Catholic household. His parents had Jesuit seminarians over for breakfast every morning. But as far as his children could see, he hated the church. He is partially deaf in one ear because the nuns, he says, were always boxing him upside the head. As a father, he dragged his children to church only because of a grinding sense of obligation. According to Lauren, the experience was awful.

Every Sunday morning, he would start getting angry in the church parking lot, and things would go downhill from there. It seemed that the family was always late. He would rush Lauren and her sister and brothers inside, hissing at them not to make any noise. If any one of them had to go to the bathroom, that was it. He would jerk all of them out of the pew and immediately go home. When the kids went to confession, he would grill them afterward. They had to tell him exactly what they'd told the priest, and then they would be punished for it. At home, they never talked about church, God, or Christianity. Being Catholic meant going to Mass. Nothing more.

The irony was that Lauren was one of those children who loved going to Mass. She told me she had visions, actual visions of angels. Jesus was her best friend for years. "But that was so long ago," she told me. "Truly, I'm overjoyed watching you discover the church. I can remember what that felt like. But I want you to remember that the Catholic path isn't for everyone."

I bristled. Here I was, walking around with my heart hanging out, and I had to listen to doubt and skepticism! I didn't want that! Yes, yes, I knew about the Inquisition and the Crusades. All those mean nuns and cruel priests. I knew a lot of cradle Catholics who grew up in pre–Vatican II days, before the reforms, and they talked about Catholic culture and how it could still be stifling, even abusive. I tried to sympathize, as much as I could, with what Lauren had gone through.

But I also knew that whenever I went to Mass, I felt waves of happiness surging inside me. I was totally, deliciously giddy. I lived for these peaks. Sometimes in church, I felt nothing at first, and I would start to panic. Then the music started, the procession would start down the aisle, and once more I couldn't breathe quite right, I was weak in the knees, and the hair stood up on my arms. I would shake my head in disbelief. How could this be happening to me? Cold, arrogant, rational, unbelieving me? I felt as if I were winning the Lotto jackpot every day. *Lord, Lord, what have I done to deserve this jackpot?*

Even as I was falling in love with the Mass, I wanted to be fair, so I tried other churches: Lutheran, Methodist, Church of Christ. I once went to a charismatic assembly, hoping for something wild and woolly, but the service, at least that day, was mild, a few well-meaning people holding their hands up in a half-filled auditorium.

One Sunday, we went to a Baptist megachurch in north Austin. I felt as though I were at a political convention. The church was huge, with seating capacity for three thousand, and plush movie-theater seats that rocked back when you sat down. There was a sense of triumph everywhere, a barrel-chested optimism that never ceased from the first howdy at the door to the last good-bye in the parking lot.

I don't want to make fun of that kind of worship—well, a part of me does—but it just wasn't for me. I missed the sweet crush of anguish that I felt in Catholic Mass. I suspected that the Mother Church had too much of a sense of the past to embrace that particular brand of all-American cheer.

Another Sunday I went to a very sweet Lutheran church. Everyone was warm and friendly and positive and welcoming, but—it just wasn't Mass. I was upset that I'd let a Sunday go by without going to Real Church. With a convert's bias, I felt that the tone of Protestant churches was just too damn perky, too "bright." Enlightenment is one of the glories of Protestantism: explaining the Scriptures, illuminating the mysteries. But I loved the darkness I found in Catholic churches. Protestants could explicate and paraphrase, and a Protestant service could be like wonderfully lucid prose. But Catholicism? Ah, that was poetry. The Mass itself was a single, unbroken poem. I needed the dark warmth, the living mystery of it all because that's where I was finding

God—in the shadows. Compared to Mass, Protestant services felt like trying to make love under fluorescent lighting.

After the Lutheran Sunday, I waited a very long week and then went to Mass at St. Mary's Cathedral. It was like sinking back into a warm bath. The words, gestures, the consecration of the Host made me melt inside. Afterward, I walked out to my car, got in, sat there for a moment in the parking lot, and then started crying. (Here we go again!) I was a little boy who had been away from his parents for two whole weeks, and I was telling myself, *I'm home again! Oh God, I'm home!*

3

Mister Toad

I've been reading *The Wind in the Willows* to my sons lately, and I see myself in Mister Toad. I've spent all my life rushing from one enthusiasm to the next. I love beginnings, fresh starts, new notebooks. When I came back from the monastery, I had found my biggest beginning yet. But I also worried that the Church was just another motorcar. Maybe two months, two years, even seven years in the future, I'd find something else, a new love, and go roaring off in yet another direction. I felt like someone on his fourth or fifth divorce. Maybe I wasn't even built for marriage.

But the thought of missing Mass, even for a Sunday, gave me a miserable feeling in the pit of my stomach that said "No! I need you!" Maybe this time was different. I thought of all my previous careers and addictions. I flew into each one with such a wild intensity, spread-eagled and full of hope. These enthusiasms were more than just hobbies; I wanted each one to be true love. But with each one I eventually crashed or sputtered out. So maybe I'd actually been looking for God all along in these things until finally, exhausted and completely whipped, I had no other option left but to find God in God himself.

Looking back, I can see that some—maybe most—of my enthusiasms were actually trying to make a religion out of things that definitely weren't.

The first clear thought I had about faith was when I was ten, talking to David, my next-door neighbor. He was six. His frog had died, and he said, a bit wistfully, "He's gone to heaven to be with Jesus," and I automatically thought, *No, he hasn't.* I wasn't arguing. I just had an immediate, gut reaction that what he said was completely wrong.

At the time, I was a little protoscientist, and "modern science" was my ideal. To me, science was a man in a white lab coat, working with test tubes and complex instruments. (And definitely a man. Science was a guy thing. The cover of my Gilbert chemistry set showed a boy and girl working on an experiment together. It was the boy who was holding up the test tube. The girl stood at his side, younger and smaller; maybe she was assisting—who knows?) These were the fifties, when science was king and scientists could be saviors, working for something larger than themselves—for Truth and the good of humankind—fighting malaria and building iron lungs.

When I was twelve, someone told me that scientists had to be good in math. I wasn't, so that ended my thoughts about a science career. Besides, emotions were becoming a problem, and a bigger one as I moved into adolescence. Science couldn't help me there. I couldn't put feelings into a test tube, and as my hormones kicked in, I had more feelings than I could manage. Depression runs in my family. You can see it in the old photographs: in my father's expression even as a child, hurt and bewildered, and also in his mother's eyes, a deep, wistful sadness that was actually very beautiful. When I was twelve, we moved to McKinney, a small town north of Dallas, and the transition was hard for me. I isolated myself and lived inside a shell. It was thick and hard, like porcelain. You could tap it with your fingernail.

And where was God in all this? God, I thought, was part of the establishment. God was church, and church was suffocation, stupidity, boredom, and everything else I was trying to escape. I groaned when my mother would announce that we were all going to church (except for Dad—he never went with us). I made every excuse I could think of: faking illness, losing my contacts, or hiding in the garage. Once we got to church, I'd sneak out to the back alley and sit on a garbage can and read.

The Sunday services were groaners, at least to me. The organ music would start up, the congregation would all rise to sing, and as soon as I stood up, waves of exhaustion flooded over me. I would stand like a limp puppet, groaning inside, my head nodding, eyes half closed, dreading the next hour. *Death! I'm surrounded by death and old people! Oxygen! I need oxygen!* I would open the hymnbook, but I refused to sing: a silent protest. *You can control my body, but you can't control my mind!* During the sermons, I would daydream, staring at the stained-glass windows. I kept fantasizing about somebody blowing holes through the windows with a shotgun. The panels would explode with a glorious shower of colored glass, and fresh air would sweep through the church, blowing over our faces, and at last I could breathe. For all the years I lived in McKinney, I never felt that I could straighten up and really breathe.

Christianity wasn't an option. As it happened, Christians—some of them—seemed to have something sweet, a peacefulness and confidence that I lacked. But I was proud of my "free thinking," and besides, Christianity required that thing called faith. Faith meant that you turned off your brain. Obviously I was too smart for that. Religion was for B students, and I made As. Besides, faith was something you were born with, like blue eyes. I had been born without a right hand, and faith was like that. I was missing parts, and I believed, quite faithfully, that faith was just another part I lacked.

◦⟡⟐⟡◦

At sixteen, with a driver's license, I could escape to Dallas, thirty
miles south. Dallas wasn't exactly the City of Lights, but compared
to McKinney, it was a window to the world. To me, McKinney was
heat and confinement. It was Old Texas, conservative and peaceful in a
deadening sort of way. Dallas was cool, literally. The whole city seemed
air conditioned. Dallas also had a new system of branch libraries in
the suburbs, and those libraries were a powerful image of everything I
wanted. The Royal Lane branch was an oxygen mask I crawled toward
every weekend, a cool, clean, well-lighted place where I could finally
calm down and read, surrounded by yards and yards of beautiful new
books in bright plastic covers.

In Dallas I discovered an art-house movie theater next to Southern
Methodist University. I went to Bergman films every few weeks. I
found a bookstore downtown that sold paperbacks by City Lights. I
read books with titles like *Unfair Arguments with Existence* and *Being
and Nothingness*. I couldn't understand them, but I liked taking them
to school. Maybe one of the girls I never had the courage to ask out
would notice the titles. I discovered *Catcher in the Rye*, the funniest
book I'd ever read. I, too, was surrounded by morons and phonies;
they were coming in the windows.

Instead of the savior scientist, I now wanted to be an "intellectual,"
whatever that was, exactly. I remember a daydream from those years. I
saw myself sitting alone in a classroom. It was the last day of the school
year. Everyone else had gone on vacation. I was at the teacher's desk
since I was a sort of teacher of nobody, and I was resting my arm on a
stack of books, a canon, all of which I'd "mastered." That was important, mastering a canon and therefore, somehow, mastering myself. I
was wearing a clean, white shirt, starched and pressed like a uniform.
All the other students had left to have fun, but I had stayed behind,

sacrificing my own pleasure to find the Truth. It was a solitary triumph, a bit lonely, but that was fine with me.

I carried this daydream with me into college, first at Southern Methodist, then at the University of Texas at Austin. I desperately wanted to be a genius. I could feel the pressure behind the bones in my forehead. *Think! Think harder!* I kept telling myself. Being really smart, I thought, was being linear, logical, and rational. But every time I tried to think in those terms, I felt dumb, like I was slogging through molasses. On top of that, I had the suspicion in the back of my mind that "rationality" only explained half the story, that logical systems were by nature a limitation, though I didn't know why.

I thought I wanted a philosophy. If I were going to be an intellectual, I needed one, right? But I read more overviews of philosophy than the philosophers themselves, and when I focused on the philosophy, I found myself more interested in the man (it was always a man) than in his books. I was always attracted to the thinker rather than the thought, more interested, that is, in what I would personally look like if I wore a particular philosophical hat. I would stand in front of the bathroom mirror, trying to develop an intelligent expression. I liked how Robert Oppenheimer looked, sort of alert and bemused at the same time, and I started smoking a pipe.

In the meantime, I lived like your usual academic monk. You can see them on any campus, hanging around the library steps on Sunday afternoons. They're never in a hurry, and they never leave. I studied seven days a week. I had a few friends, who usually were my girlfriends. Like Woody Allen, I'd always preferred the conversation of women to men. Women made sense. They were right, somehow, and I felt they had something I lacked. But none of the relationships lasted. Sooner or later, I retreated back to the library.

So again, where was God? Being very patient, I think. I was somewhat spiritually ambitious. I read books about Zen. Zen was cool.

Besides, it was Eastern. Western religions were definitely less cool, less intellectually respectable. Besides, I still felt that religion was for B students.

And Christians? Christians were a walking embarrassment. They were well-meaning people with tender hearts and soft brains who settled for easy answers. Sometimes they would approach me on campus. I'd be taking a break outside the library, a sitting duck. Suddenly I'd see an evangelical type approaching me with a sweet, friendly smile that made my skin crawl. I felt as if I were being panhandled. Usually it was a young man in a white, short-sleeve shirt with a skinny black tie. Instantly, I'd throw out a mental force field—*Go away! Shoo! Scat!* Maybe if I looked hostile enough, he'd get the message. But he never did. He would introduce himself and then politely ask—I would sigh—if I'd ever heard about Jesus. Sometimes they gave me little pamphlets with schematic drawings showing GOD at the top, MAN at the bottom, and JESUS as a bunch of little arrows rising up like bean sprouts, connecting the two.

At this point, I usually got up and left. Years later, I would learn the difference between a simple-minded faith (what I thought this was) and a faith of simplicity (what they might have had, for all I knew). Actually I was the one reducing things to stick figures. If Christianity was the cartoon I thought it was, I wouldn't have to think about it at all. And faith? Faith was lobotomy, pure and simple.

Still, something was missing. I slogged through philosophies, frustrated and hungry. I felt that I was living inside a sort of gray fog, an out-of-focus drizzle that kept me from seeing what I could only think of as "Truth." This Truth was like a clear, logical gridwork but with a "meaning" that surrounded it like a neon glow. Truth was both the gridwork and the glow, both clarity and something beyond. I remember a painting by Walter Tandy Murch that I thought was mysterious and wonderful. It was a still life of a carburetor, painted in dark brown tones but with a beautiful shimmer so that it seemed to glow from within. That was an image of the kind of Truth I was looking for: logical and exact but alive with a resonance I couldn't explain.

Though I didn't know it then, I think I was looking for a sacramental vision—the divine incarnated in the physical world. In the meantime, I kept reading my Zen books. I learned how enlightenment struck when you finally understood the essence in a bowl of tea, so I stared at my coffee mug. I meditated. I typed out a passage from George Eliot's *Middlemarch* and taped it to my refrigerator:

> If we had a keen vision and feeling of all ordinary human life, it would be like hearing the grass grow and the squirrel's heart beat, and we should die of that roar which lies on the other side of silence.

I felt that something was thundering over our lives every second of the day, but I couldn't hear it. Living inside a porcelain shell didn't help, of course. I didn't want to find logic in emotion so much as emotion in logic. What appealed was the possibility of true passion in thinking, the poetry of an engineer, the scientist I wanted to be as a boy, who underneath all that seriousness really had true feelings and was fully human. But being human meant breaking open my shell, and I wasn't ready for that quite yet.

After four years of college, I had only a vague sense of interconnectedness leading to a vague sense of responsibility about being decent, and a vague sense of accepting the universe. Not very impressive, but it was what I had, and would have, for the next thirty years. I saw thousands of pieces, but no way to fit them together.

I went to Berkeley to work on a Ph.D. because, well, why not? Maybe I could be an English professor. Besides, the alternative was leaving the only world where I had been a success, and I wasn't ready to leave it.

I had done well at the University of Texas, but at Berkeley, my own little lightbulb of achievement was lost in the collective brilliance of a mob of grad students who had all been stars in their own undergraduate departments. I'd made Phi Beta Kappa? Well, who hadn't? I stumbled through my first year in a daze.

By spring semester, I felt like a cloud of scattered dots. I was losing myself. I was nothing more than average, and that was intolerable. My ambition to become an intellectual had led me nowhere. "I need something that nobody can take away from me," I remember saying to a friend. So I decided, very consciously and deliberately, to become a poet.

I could have become a novelist, but these were the days before word processors. Novelists have to do a lot of typing, and with only one hand and a cheap typewriter, I couldn't see myself pounding out those heavy manuscripts. Lyric poems would be easier to type. (I know, that's not very romantic. You're supposed to write poems because you're called by the muse of poetry, but somebody has to do the paper-work.) Besides, poetry seemed to be much more subjective. I could retreat—and that's the operative word here—into a highly subjective process where my work, I thought, would be harder for others to judge. I was surprised that even the big names in the department were often reluctant to talk about a poem written by somebody who was still alive. So from the beginning, poetry was an escape for me, a way to retreat from the world and all its assessments.

I mention the poetry because it's a part of my story but also because it prepared me later on for a Catholic way of thinking—both right and left brain, both faith and reason. When I first started writing, I was drawn to two Roberts: Lowell and Bly. Lowell was a writer that an English major could understand. I could see how he had written a line and then gone back and jacked up each word until everything was bristling with multilayered meanings and verbal power. As he himself said, he wanted his poems to look as if they had been hard to write.

That satisfied the American work ethic in me. With patience and study, I could unpack the poems, see how Lowell did it, and try it myself. The poems gave the impression of "tremendous power under tremendous pressure," very masculine, I thought, very much East Coast intellectual. *Lord Weary's Castle* was brilliant on every page. (It was written while he was a Catholic, but that didn't concern me then.) The book was exactly what I wanted: eccentric, unique, all its own, but still very much poetry that recognized the literary and academic establishment. Lowell had gone to Harvard and blazed his own trail, outshining everyone. Heavens, he'd won the Pulitzer with his first book. He was the ultimate successful schoolboy.

Then a girlfriend showed me some books by Robert Bly. Over the weekend I read a few, then a few more. I was "stunned by degrees," to quote Dickinson. By Monday morning I was a different person. My mind had been a busy machine with Lowell, but with Bly, it rolled to a stop and started humming lightly. As I read the poems in *Silence in the Snowy Fields*, I realized I'd never, ever seen anything like this poetry before:

> The barn is full of corn, and moving toward us now,
> Like a hulk blown toward us in a storm at sea;
> All the sailors on deck have been blind for many years.

These lines were more than strange. They were from another universe of understanding. They were stranger than anything the San Francisco poets or the Beats had written. They encouraged, demanded a new way of thinking that wasn't irrational so much as profoundly arational.

They tapped lobes in my animal brain I never knew existed:

> We are approaching sleep: the chestnut blossoms in the mind
> Mingle with thoughts of pain

And the long roots of barley, bitterness
As of the oak roots staining the waters dark
in Louisiana, the wet streets soaked with rain
And sodden blossoms, out of this
We have come, a tunnel softly hurtling into darkness.

Deep image was the term used for poetry like this. Bly was part of a generation influenced by South American and European poets who wrote poems that seemed quiet and simple but that undercut all the logical, scientific, and cultural structures of Western rationality. This was a long way from the test-tube science I'd admired as a boy. There was nothing muddy or vague about this poetry. It was very precise, but it was a precision of mood and tone. The ideas were conveyed as emotions rather than as logical arguments or abstract distinctions. For the first time I found that I could truly appreciate writing that I couldn't understand and I could understand what I couldn't explain.

If Truth was a paradox, then here was a way to embody it. Here was that gridwork with a neon glow I'd been thinking about. Almost all poems had some sort of structure or argument or flow, however loose, from one image to the next, something we can paraphrase. That paraphrase was the gridwork. At the same time, of course, a poem is always more than its paraphrase. It's all the connotations, the unconscious suggestions, allusions, associations, and glimmers of ideas "glowing" around the gridwork. Poetry was a way to understand in two ways, with both the head and the heart.

David Tracy talks about what he calls the Catholic "analogical imagination," a metaphorical way of thinking based on "both/and" rather than "either/or." Catholicism honors rationality, but it's still a religion that rides on the poetic language of metaphor. The Mass, as I said, is a poem from beginning to end. The angels and saints are very real poems. The Eucharist itself is a poem in which metaphors become literal, literally joining the divine and natural worlds. Anything sacramental requires a poetic understanding to even approach that mystery. Poetry was never a religion to me, but it helped prepare me for the religion I needed.

⌒∞⌒

If I found a refuge in poetry while at Berkeley, I also found a refuge in drinking. With me, poetry and drinking were good friends, and over the years, they developed a faithful and destructive relationship. Each one made the other seem attractive. Each fed off the weaknesses in the other, using those weaknesses as a self-consuming strength.

The drinking helped my narcissism, and the poetry helped justify the drinking. Everyone knew about the myth of the tormented, Romantic poet, somebody like Baudelaire—it was always Baudelaire—who wrote brilliant poems between sips of absinthe. No matter that the greatest writers were not self-destructive. Was Shakespeare a drunk? Was Homer an addict? I didn't answer that question. I knew I could just drink and keep writing from inside my shell. I drank my way through graduate school, then drank my way out. Maybe it gave me the false courage—which was better than no courage at all—to leave.

For years I enjoyed the life of a grad student. I enjoyed the intellectual atmosphere, but I enjoyed even more not having to get a real job. I enjoyed the minor prestige of being a teaching associate with my own section, and I "dated" several of my students. I was independent of most middle-class worries. My parents kept sending me checks to supplement my income; I could work at my own pace, and I lived a quiet life at the end of a cul-de-sac in a duplex apartment on the banks of Strawberry Creek.

After seven years I had worked and drunk myself to a standstill. I was getting nowhere with my dissertation. My chapters kept getting too philosophical. I was trying to explain How Poetry Works instead of choosing a manageable thesis and defending it. I knew I was burned out with school. I didn't want to be a scholar and didn't want to be a critic. I just wanted to write poetry. I didn't have to get up in the morning and go dragging off to a job, but I knew my life was artificial and subsidized. Time was running out.

One morning I was eating breakfast and listening to the sounds of construction in the lot next door. Everyone seemed very busy over there. A new nursing home was going up, and I could hear pounding and men yelling over the sound of heavy machinery. I felt safe inside my little world. My own backyard was completely walled off with a huge, living fence of blackberry brambles, well over six feet high, so large it spilled over into the other lot. I had always felt secure behind that living barricade in a neighborhood where people needed bars over their windows.

Suddenly I saw the blade of a bulldozer rising up behind the wall of brambles. I watched dumbfounded as the blade tore through the wall of thorns and dragged it away. In a few minutes, the fence was gone. I remembered my landlady once telling me there had been a dispute about the property line. My backyard, my home, everything was now completely exposed to the world. It was like something out of a dream.

Omen, I thought. I had definitely been too long at the fair.

In fact, I can tell you the exact moment when I knew I was finished with grad school. I was sitting in the School of Education library, surrounded by kiddie-lit books like *The Little Engine That Could* and *Where the Wild Things Are*. I was struggling once again with the first chapter of my dissertation, talking about poems and their paraphrases. After twenty minutes, I sighed and looked around at all those studious education majors, and I thought, *I'm never going to finish this dissertation. Never, ever.*

For a moment, I sat there. And then I felt someone beside me, and that someone went all the way back to my childhood, back through years of grinding work and competitive worry, through grad school and undergraduate courses, back through the anxieties of high school, junior high, and primary school, all the way back to Mrs. Abbott's first grade class at Ridglea Hills Elementary School in Ft. Worth, Texas, to a little boy in the back row with a knot in his stomach. And the invisible someone tapped that boy gently on the shoulder and whispered, "School's over. You can go now. You're free."

The next day, I resigned from grad school. I celebrated by packing the car and driving cross-country to visit a buddy in Iowa. Then I visited my parents back in Texas and announced I was leaving school.

My parents were stunned. They'd always had doubts about an English degree. My father had suffered a massive stroke the year before, and they truly didn't need this crap. He struggled to sit up in bed. "What about your future?" he asked me in an angry, quaking voice, as loud as he could before collapsing back into the pillows. Quietly I told them they would just have to have faith in their son. I was going to be a poet.

They pointed out how much money they had paid for my education. They talked about careers and other options. But I wasn't listening. The next morning, they watched me go back to California, where I would finish out my last year of teaching. I wasn't good at arguing, but I was very good at leaving.

Many years later, I attended the funeral of a friend's mother. As final words were said over the casket, I watched some of her grandsons standing in the first row. They were awkward, decent young men who represented the next generation and hope of that family. I think I understood then something of what my parents had felt that day when I walked out the door. They were truly trying to help, and they were probably feeling not so much anger as a miserable sense of waste. I was throwing away a career for a few measly lines of verse. By the time I stood at that funeral, both of my parents had passed away. It has taken me most of an adult life to realize what I did to my parents and any last hopes they had for me.

Back at Berkeley, I looked at a map of the United States. Minneapolis seemed like a good bet. I was thinking about writing a novel about Robert Scott, the polar explorer, and I wanted to go someplace cold. I also thought that Minneapolis would have a decent library system.

I was scared witless to be finally leaving the womb. Over the years, I'd created a life as a professional student. I had many keys on my chain: an office key, a study carrel key, the English Department building key, and three keys to libraries. I could walk through so many doors on that campus. But now, after moving out of my apartment, I had only the key to my Volkswagen. I also had a strong taste of defeat in my mouth. True, I really wanted to be a writer, and I was off to seek my literary fortune. But underneath that excitement was the fear that I might be on my way to another failure.

In Minneapolis I got a part-time job in a liquor store and wrote poems every morning. In the evening, I read about polar exploration.

I never wrote that book about Scott, how he died struggling to return from the South Pole, but the polar expeditions became a personal mythology. The explorers were heroes of a very special kind, brave men pushing their bodies beyond their limits, as if they had no bodies, as if they were immortal. Apsley Cherry-Garrard, a companion of Scott, once wrote, "Exploration is the physical expression of an intellectual passion."

Yes! I thought when I read that. What's more, the idea of undergoing enormous pain, exhaustion, and danger to reach an invisible, mathematical point on a map had a gloriously insane quality that thrilled me.

These men, especially the ones like Scott who died, were my martyr saints, the closest I could get to religion. I wasn't surprised when I read that polar explorers were like desert explorers; both often had a strong streak of mysticism. I was fascinated by the idea of cold and absolute zero. Deep subzero was a different world, a beautifully hellish place where steel shattered like glass and a candle burned down through a tube of wax because the outside of the candle was too cold to melt. Absolute zero was like zero latitude at the poles, the ultimate still point in a moving world, and I thought that reaching minus 459.67 degrees Fahrenheit, the coldest cold there was, would be like touching God.

Walking along Hennepin Avenue in Minneapolis in the dead of January with a wind chill of thirty below, I saw myself trekking across my own private wasteland, marching toward a personal idea of poetry and Truth. One winter, I tried to spend a few weeks in a cabin beside a frozen lake north of Duluth, though I found myself driving into town every morning for pancakes just to be around clattering dishes and people's voices. But I always found my polar wasteland on the blank page.

That page was often barren. I once read about sled dogs on the high Antarctic plains. After days on the snowfields, they became so famished for physical, sensory detail that they got a little crazy if they saw anything at all that was dark and specific, even a rock the size of a football, a mile away. They would race for the rock and then stand around barking and sniffing and fighting over it until they were pulled away by brute force. Looking back through my notebooks from those years, I realize now I was like those dogs, moving deeper and deeper into vacancy, famished for something—anything—to bark about. I never found much, but I would set out at dawn every morning, leaving family, friends, lovers, a future, and everything else behind me. That was the way you lived as a poet, I thought. You bet your life.

In reality, of course, there was nothing heroic about how I lived. I thought Minneapolis would be a good place to dry out from my drinking days in California. Instead, the drinking only increased. I careened in and out of a disastrous love affair with a sad, beautiful woman who was also alcoholic. When she told me that, yes, she was going to get married, but not to me, I spun out of control. I woke up in strange places for a while.

I finally ran through my savings. I figured I could write, so I found a job as a copywriter in advertising. For the next year, I worked hundred-hour weeks to learn the trade. During that same period, I drank a quart or more of liquor every day. I would drive to work in the morning with a coffee cup of bourbon on the dashboard—I thought that was extremely cool—and drink a pint before I got to work, just to get normal. Then I'd drink another pint in the evening, then go out to the bars.

The more I drank, the harder I worked. Some days, I felt as if the air itself was bruising my skin. I would roll out of bed and lie there for a long, long time, then crawl slowly around the room on my hands and knees for the next twenty minutes. I would be so depressed I had trouble breathing, much less standing up.

All this anguish was fascinating, of course. I was rubbernecking at my own car crash. A part of me wanted to see how far I could push the edge. What's more, my life was wonderfully simplified: you simply drank as much as you could while still keeping your job. I was living for a habit which was truly bigger than me. Drinking seemed like a noble calling.

One winter evening I was parked beside Lake Nokomis in Minneapolis. It must have been twenty below, and I was drinking a pint of brandy. I'd been drinking quite a bit for most of a year, and I remember being vaguely aware that I was going down, approaching some sort of absolute point. Not there yet, but getting close.

In the dark, staring into a snow bank, I asked myself, *Is this hell?* and slowly the thought gelled in my mind: *Hell is boring.* Hmm, that was interesting. This had never occurred to me. I thought that hell might be agony, but maybe hell was where you were just bored for eternity. Which would finally be agony.

I realized that I wasn't thrilled any longer with walking on the edge. Self-destruction was, to be honest, boring. It would still be years before I finally pulled myself together, but over the next several months, I drank less and eventually stopped altogether for as long as I lived in Minneapolis. I became what twelve-step programs call a "dry drunk." I didn't drink, but I never changed inside. In classic fashion, I thought my will was bigger than alcohol. "I can do it myself!" said the inner child. I drank coffee all day while I wrote, then took sleeping pills every night to sleep. Finally, it was only a tiny pink fragment of a pill, wrapped in a tissue in my jeans pocket, but I carried it with me everywhere and never missed a night without taking it. The pill was my roaring addiction, now reduced to a tiny ember but always at hand, ready to flare up again.

As I drank less, I started long-distance running. Running, especially marathons, fit in nicely with my polar myth. Here was another glorious attempt involving endurance and pain in the service of a goal that defied all common sense. I had an image in my mind: an "incandescent runner" racing across the polar wasteland, running toward pure light until he somehow broke into flames. I watched the movie *Chariots of Fire* several times. At one point, the Eric Liddell character, a champion runner from Scotland who later became a missionary in

China, says, "I believe God made me for a purpose, but he also made me fast. And when I run I feel his pleasure." My heart soared when I heard that. I wanted to feel that pleasure.

After several years in Minneapolis, I had managed to cobble together a writer's life. Half the time I lived on grants and made steady progress on my first book of poems. I let people into my life only if they could serve my writing. I chose my girlfriends for their emotional safety. If I had to choose a single image that represented my twenties and early thirties, it would be a woman saying good-bye as I went out the door, saying good-bye in airports and bus depots, and waving good-bye in the rearview mirror as I drove away.   .

If I worshipped anything at all, it was my ego, and I justified this worship in the name of art. Yes, yes, I know I'm sounding like the repentant convert here, but honestly, folks, I think back on those days, and I can't be proud. I used people. People began to look at me sideways and edge away.

I knew that I'd reached another dead end. For five years I had sifted through every little tic and feeling, every nuance, idea, and intuition in my psyche, and I'd finally come up with forty pages of poetry. Now the book was finished, and I was thirty-three. What next?

In therapy they sometimes talk about "doing a geographical." Patients try to solve their problems by changing their zip code. Maybe if I moved on, something would kick loose. After all, that's what I had done when I moved from California to Minneapolis, or from Texas to California for that matter.

I looked at the map again and decided to go to New York. I had always been afraid of the city, but the previous year I had visited Manhattan. I walked around the streets for a few days and survived. Standing on the corner of Fifth Avenue and 59th Street, I decided "the axis of the world ground through Central Park." New York was the big leagues, the natural next step for the successful writer I obviously was.

Then I met Lauren.

⌒∞∞⌒

The Seattle area is a dark green, complicated landscape. Its underlying geology of sediment folded between fault lines is so complex that it's never been mapped with complete accuracy. It's not a landscape you can step back and observe. Rather, you have to enter the deep forests and wander around and even get lost before you really understand where you are.

Lauren spent her first years in Seattle, beside the edge of the forest. Her earliest memories were rain and the mists rising off Puget Sound. When I met her, she seemed to radiate soft lushness and amplitude, as she still does to me. I was all knobby brittleness, like a desert plant. I'd grown up on the flat, baked prairies in North Texas. I held her and realized how parched I'd been. She was like water to me, and at night she would sigh and run her hands over my body, and her hands felt like water. I was sinking into warm pools, and the tiny bits and slivers of polar ice in my heart began to melt. This is what I'd been looking for all my life.

She was, and is, beautiful like only those people who are unaware of their beauty. Growing up, she felt so unattractive that she always made friends with the blind students at school, eating lunch at their cafeteria table because she knew they couldn't see what she looked like.

When I looked at her myself, I saw a tall, lovely woman with dark hair and a low, soft voice. She would talk to me very quietly on the telephone like an FM announcer late at night, and I was weak in the knees. Beyond that, she was a balance that I'd been looking for. Every other girlfriend I'd known was either bright and practical or darkly self-destructive. The cheerfulness was soon boring. The darkness was powerful, rich, and erotic, but it led to catastrophe. With one or the other, I felt that my life would go so far and no further. But Lauren was a balance, and I couldn't see an end to what we would find together.

I amazed myself. I had been resisting middle-class norms for years, but suddenly here I was, all my instincts tingling, a salmon thrashing upstream through a hundred miles of raging water to spawn. I asked her to marry me, and yes, she said yes.

Was this just another enthusiasm? I was worried at the time that it might be. But if God gave me enthusiasms, with Lauren he also gave me love. The difference was that with Lauren, I didn't have a choice. Enthusiasms can divert us, but they never overwhelm us except in a flat, obsessive sort of way. Enthusiasms turn into love when you realize that you're not the one who's driving anymore. Love takes you gently but very firmly by the neck. I was never overwhelmed by the other women I'd known—which was why I chose them. My indifference made me safe. Even my poetry wasn't true love. I could have lived without it. Perhaps that's why I never wrote any better than I did. It was something I chose, but it didn't choose me.

What I felt for Lauren was indeed true love. It felt as though I were being turned inside out, becoming a part of something that was more than just more of me. Besides, I knew that somehow it was meant to be. I was in Minneapolis only because I'd looked at a map. She was there because she'd filled in the wrong zip code when she applied to college. She had intended to go to St. Mary's in Louisiana but wound up at St. Mary's in Minnesota. After college, she moved to Minneapolis, and then we found each other just weeks before she was moving to LA and I was leaving for New York. What are the odds of our meeting like that and getting married? A billion to one? At this point, I can only explain it as someone's plan.

4

Praying to the Radiator

New York City is a great place to learn. The first thing Lauren and I learned was that we weren't the geniuses we thought we were. When we arrived, we simply assumed we were going to be famous. I would write poetry that captured the epic dimensions of twentieth-century New York. Lauren was going to be a brilliant filmmaker. Simply having a Manhattan zip code encouraged this kind of thinking. After all, you lived just blocks away from important celebrities. Career lightning was striking everywhere—no reason not to assume that a stray bolt would hit you as well.

Nothing happened, the years went by, and still nothing happened. I got a job working in an ad agency, writing brochures for IBM. Lauren struggled to find work. For the first time, I was financially responsible for someone other than myself, and I handled it poorly. I wrote in the odd hours, and resented having to work at all.

Like Lauren, I was terrified. I kept having what I called the Elevator Feeling: You walk into a business meeting or maybe just an expensive bar or restaurant, and suddenly you realize that you're in way over your head, and your stomach drops and you feel like you're in an elevator rushing up to the sky. Eventually, we learned to handle ourselves better, but we were always outsmarted, outgunned, and outclassed by the big guys.

I started drinking again. All it took was a casual suggestion one night, the tip of a finger. From then on, Lauren and I had miserable arguments fueled by bourbon, yelling so loudly that the downstairs neighbor would pound on his ceiling with a broom handle until we stopped, humiliated and out of breath.

In time, we adjusted to our life together. Lauren found a job. I wrote during the weekends. But New York wasn't ever the grand adventure we had expected. I enjoyed a few successes. My poems were published here and there in the literary magazines.

Then my first book, *The Glass Children*, was accepted by a university press. When it came out, I expected the traffic in Manhattan to stop, people reading my book on every street corner, millions staying home from work to savor every line. Congratulations would pour in, and the telephone would start ringing constantly as a grateful and astonished world beat a path to my door.

As it was, the book was reviewed twice, then disappeared from the face of the earth. Like many other less-than-best-selling authors, I wanted to put the cover on milk cartons: "Have You Seen This Book?" By the time I was approaching my forties, I was finishing my second book of poetry, *Success Stories*, but I felt that old feeling, the one I had with graduate studies, of hitting another colossal dead end.

As the years went by, I even developed a growing suspicion of poetry itself. I had tried to make a religion out of art, to join the church of Walt Whitman. But I also wanted poetry to show us the Truth, and I had come to believe that Truth was somehow beyond poetry and all the rhetoric of art. I kept writing, but the fire inside was fading.

Then in 1988, my father died. I started feeling that maybe it was time to grow up. I was almost forty. I couldn't drink the way I used to. I started having hangovers every morning. I tried switching to beer, then wine, then back to bourbon, but nothing helped. I had the growing sense of red lights on the dashboard that I couldn't ignore. If I continued like this, my life would truly go nowhere, or worse.

A fellow copywriter saw the obvious and took me out to lunch one day. She told me that she was in a twelve step program and suggested that I check it out. I didn't argue. Actually, I was relieved that somebody had finally noticed.

I stopped drinking and started going to meetings. In fact, all winter I went to meetings, mainly on Fourteenth Street, in a quiet room in the back of an office building. Through the windows I could see the scrawny branches of an ailanthus tree. Month after month I sat in meetings, listening to stories and telling mine. I read my literature and went to meetings. I made new friends and "worked my program." Winter moved into spring, and slowly the ailanthus began to bud, and by early summer it was dark green and thick with leaves.

I've noticed that whatever we expect in our lives usually happens, but it takes a lot longer than expected. That was the way the program worked. One of the main lessons I learned was that in recovery you're actually doing two things: First, you stop drinking. That's the easy part, in a way. It has to do with not bending your elbow. You just don't pick up a drink. Second, you Get Sober. That part takes the rest of your life because you're literally changing who you are from the ground up. Getting Sober is why people go to meetings year after year. There's no end and no rushing it.

I discovered that when I'd been drinking, I was *always* under the influence, always deluded, even the next morning when I thought I was "sober." Now my life was coming into focus, and suddenly details jumped out with overwhelming clarity. I felt as if a huge, long overdue credit-card bill had been dumped on my doorstep. I was answering the doorbell every morning and finding a long line of creditors, each one with a list of what I had screwed up or failed to do. I went through all the classic stages of Getting Sober, from the initial pink-cloud honeymoon period to the wincing stage and then to the cringing stage. I started to remember all those stupid, idiotic things I'd done in the past, most often when I thought I was being witty.

I became a regular in the program. I set up the folding chairs, I made coffee, I got a sponsor, and I chaired meetings. I did what people told me to do. If they'd told me to stick a banana in my ear, I would have done it. I had tried to stop drinking by myself, had tried a hundred times. Now I surrendered to the program with a kind of relief. Lauren also stopped drinking. She never went to very many meetings—I carped at her for a while—but as long as she didn't drink, that was fine with me.

So what did I learn from the Twelve Steps?

I learned, or began to learn, a sense of moderation, though the alcohol had to be stopped entirely. "Drunks have two speeds," I was told. "A hundred miles per hour, and fuck-it." You might think that drunks are lazy people who could care less, but a lot of us are perfectionists. It's all or nothing. That's sometimes why we drink, to escape that insatiable, niggling perfectionism, at least for a while. Perfectionism can also be a form of anger, and anger is a classic alcoholic emotion.

I learned patience. I learned that change, real change, often took years. Three years wasn't a long time to be in the program. People were still learning the basics after twenty.

I learned to be skeptical about my enthusiasms. When I first entered the program, I thought the best members were the obvious ones, the ones who talked the most in meetings. Only years later did I recognize the true children of light. They didn't say much, but when they did, it mattered. Most important, they were always there, and always with the person who needed help the most. My own gusto now seemed suspiciously close to self-centeredness—Hey, look at me! The one with all the right attitudes! I tried to replace those initial flashes with the warm, steady light that I saw coming from the older members.

I learned that self-loathing was a false virtue and simply another form of self-centeredness. And guilt isn't the same as humility. I needed to admit my wrongs and make restitution but then get on with my life. Otherwise I would be caught in a rut, going over the same issues—which is actually a major hallmark of addiction, why they call it a habit.

I learned to demystify the image of the doomed, self-destructive poet, the Romantic hero, tormented and solitary. Enough of that.

I learned how trivial my problems were. Viktor Frankl survived being a prisoner in a Nazi concentration camp. He said that our sufferings are like gas released in a room: regardless of the quantity, the gas expands to meet the limits of the room. Big troubles, little troubles, all feel the same to us in the room called "my life." I thought I had suffered, sort of. But my own life story was a paper cut compared to the sagas I heard in the program.

I met people who had woken up in a hospital bed the morning after, handcuffed to the railing. People with foot-long scars I didn't even ask about. People who had been on a first-name basis with the ER staff because they had their stomach pumped almost every weekend. People who had almost died, over and over again.

One fellow told me about living in a squat in Harlem, a caved-in tenement with sections of the floor missing. He rolled out of bed one morning and fell two stories to the basement. "Rude awakening" was a common theme in those meetings. I once added up the number of people I'd met in the program who'd been shot because they were in the wrong place at the wrong time, and it was over a dozen.

I also learned that for me, nothing ever changes until I go to a room and sit down with other warm bodies and interact in some way.

I gotta show up, I gotta serve, and I gotta talk. I usually went to a meeting in a church basement a few blocks away from our apartment. For the first two years, every time I walked up to the basement door, I was hoping that the meeting had been cancelled. But the door was always unlocked. Even then, I sometimes just snuck in, listened silently, and left as soon as possible. But I learned that I had to schmooze with somebody, even for a few minutes. Otherwise the meeting didn't "work" and I was depressed the next day. Service was the same way. Making coffee for the meeting was enlightened self-interest.

Finally, I learned to pray, or pray as best I could. The second step, "Came to believe that a power greater than ourselves could restore us to sanity," is a biggie, and people found all sorts of ways to take that step. One man said that when he began the program, he prayed to the radiator in his basement apartment. Why not? It was bolted to the ceiling, so it was something from above. It was solid and dependable, and it kept him warm through the New York winters. Another member told us how she first started praying to a lightbulb. "Fake It Till You Make It" is a popular slogan, and we learned that it's okay to go through the motions, because often the heart and mind will follow.

I looked around for my own radiator. Going to church wasn't an option for me. The idea was simply too outlandish. I still thought religion was for B students. The closest I could get was the rough-and-ready philosophy of recovery. What did it matter if the sayings were so simple you could put them on bumper stickers? Lives were being saved in those rooms. Besides, I was finding that I wasn't as complex as I thought I was.

One day, walking across Ninth Street in Brooklyn, I looked around and realized that "Higher Power" could also be "Larger Power," that God could be simply the larger world around me. It lacked any sense of transcendence, but it was a start.

I went to a member, a gentleman from the South Bronx, and asked him how to pray. "Hit those knees," he said.

"Knees?"

"Get on your knees," he explained patiently. "Here. You put your hands together like this, see? Then you talk to your Higher Power. Sometimes you listen. Maybe listen more than talk. It's real simple."

After that, whenever I met him in the meetings, he'd ask me, "Hittin' those knees?" So I did, just like he told me. At first it felt strange, as if it were happening to someone else, as if I were doing something really bizarre, like wearing women's underwear. But in time, I found that I liked it quite a bit—the praying that is.

I spent years in the program, going the whole nine yards: making my meetings, cleaning up, fixing coffee, acting as chairperson. But as time went by, I felt that once again, something more was needed. The program is profoundly spiritual, but it's not a church, and it doesn't call itself a religion. I wanted a path I could follow. I wanted a creed. I still hadn't found anything that made sense. I was still hungry.

It wasn't just a matter of faith or not. By then I had realized that everybody takes something on faith. Even skepticism takes itself on faith as a methodology, the best one, presumably, for arriving at the truth. And science? Great for some things, but the scientific worldview starts to buckle once we try to explain the really big questions about ultimate meanings. What's the purpose of life? Where did we come from? Why are we here? Where are we going? Science has answers but only in scientific terms. Scientists are always at the mercy of their instruments. A heart monitor can't tell me what it means to be human.

As I continued with the program, I dabbled and picked through the long buffet table of spirituality. I sat with Zen priests in their quiet temples. I admired their compassion, but Buddhism seemed too detached, too up in the head. Where's the passion, I wondered, but to Buddhists, passion was a part of the problem. I went to Scientology meetings, but the Scientologists were all wigged out and paranoid. I danced with New Age "moon dancers" who met once a month in the woods and beat drums and spun around in big circles. I felt foolish. We all seemed like just a bunch of suburban white kids trying to act like Druids.

I sniffed around witchcraft and the occult. I attended a Samhain celebration one Halloween; we lit candles and chanted something about fertility. For a while I hung around a shop on Twelfth Street filled with occult books and paraphernalia. This wasn't eco-friendly Druidism; it was black magic. The store was dark and creepy. Just inside the front door was an apple crate filled with human skulls. (Yes, you *can* buy anything in New York.) The owner sat behind the counter with a huge, mastiff guard dog at his feet. Both of them watched me closely, not moving.

I heard about black masses and attended some, but I decided that you could take them seriously only if you were somehow Catholic—that is, if you took the real Masses seriously as well. With my Methodist background, the whole thing seemed silly. In fact, the occult thing in general seemed silly.

Lauren was still a practicing Catholic back then, and she patiently watched me go through these changes and experiments. Years later when I was trying to drag her to Mass, she reminded me that she had tried to do the same thing with me back in New York. I remember once walking with her across Central Park when we first lived in the city, feeling superior and irritated as she talked about God and faith. I told her I wasn't a Christian, I simply wasn't spiritual. "Of course you're spiritual," she said. "You're built for it." I didn't know what to say.

The closest I came to joining a church was when I attended Quaker meetings in Brooklyn. I admired the Quakers hugely. Like the monks at Corpus Christi, they simply accepted my presence. No fuss. No evangelizing. Every Sunday I would walk to the meeting house in Brooklyn Heights and enter a large, upper room that was filled with light. The room was simple, even Zenlike. There was nothing I could object to: no cross, no religious images or signs anywhere. Just a large room filled with pews facing each other and the Sunday morning light streaming through the high windows.

At the beginning of every meeting, someone would make a few remarks, and then we would all sit very still. The silence would gather around us and deepen and grow throughout the hour. If anyone had the impulse to speak, they stood up, spoke for a little while, and then sat down. More silence. Sometimes the comments would be unrelated to each other. Other times, a thread was established as each person took up the thought and carried it forward. Many times, I felt a spirit alive in that room. After an hour, the meeting was gently brought to a close. Many times I had the impulse to get up and speak. I wanted to stand up and simply say, "Thank you." Then "Thank you. Thank you." But I was shy and never did.

I read Quaker writers and admired their respect for the "common and obscure duties" of life. I respected their history of commitment. Lauren and I once visited a cemetery on Shelter Island where Quakers were buried, executed for their faith. I also admired the way Quakers conducted their business meetings for the church. Like the services, the meetings would begin in silence. People would stand up and speak their piece. If a debate began, everyone could have their say, and— I was floored by this—if anyone felt that they truly needed to repeat their point, they would apologize first before doing so.

I almost, almost joined the Quakers. I teetered and hemmed and hawed, but at the last minute I finally drew back. After a few more months, I stopped going to meetings. I had various excuses. But to be honest, I think I just didn't have the courage to take that last step. Or maybe I wasn't ready or humble or desperate enough. Or maybe God could see that it just wasn't working out between me and the Quakers. I was turning into a Holy Joe, gently chiding people—my wife for example—for their New York manners. Then people—my wife for example—soon pointed out the limits of this behavior in terms blunt enough for even me to understand.

"The program saved my life." I heard that from hundreds of members as the years went by. I don't know if it saved my own life, but I know for sure that it saved me for a better one. When Lauren and I stopped drinking, we suddenly realized that we weren't living in a hip neighborhood. We were in fact living in a very expensive designer slum, with everything infected with graffiti and heroin. Funny how we'd missed that.

We moved almost immediately out of Manhattan to a pleasant street in Brooklyn. We slept, truly slept, at night for the first time in years. Our marriage improved. Lauren became pregnant. Our prayed-for child, a son, arrived safely. Regardless of what sort of father I am, I hate to think what kind I would have been with a drink in my hand.

In Brooklyn, I kept going to meetings every week. I met some of the kindest, wisest, and most generous people I have ever known. Also some of the biggest jerks, though everyone seemed to get better as time went on, even the ones I thought would never make it, myself included.

One evening I was sitting in the church basement waiting for the meeting to begin. I looked around me and for a moment felt as though I were looking through the wrong end of a telescope. The whole room seemed very distant, and I had the sense that I would know exactly what was going to be said. Yes, I think I "got it." And yes, I knew for sure that "it" applied to me. But I had my old feeling of needing more. The program wasn't a religion; the meetings weren't church. I prayed, but there was still an emptiness inside. I had to do something, though. Otherwise I would slip back into depression or worse.

I found myself thinking about t'ai chi, the slow-motion exercise they do in China. Sometimes in the morning I would walk to work through Chinatown. The parks would be filled with hundreds of people rising and slowly spinning under the trees. They were lovely. I watched a teacher go through Crane Standing on One Leg, and his body was like moving granite, geologic in its power, yet every part was perfectly and wonderfully fluid. Whether I knew it or not, this was sacramental movement, an invisible, spiritual energy expressed in physical form.

T'ai chi was quiet, peaceful, and strong, and it was very beautiful. Whatever Truth was, I knew it was beautiful. Not easy, maybe, but beautiful. I looked through Manhattan for a teacher, went through several courses, then found Ernie in Brooklyn. I studied with the man for two years. Very slowly—like anything that counts—he taught us the basic form. Ernie had learned it from Sat Chuen Hon who had learned it from ninety-four-year-old Master Ku who had developed the form while living in Taoist monasteries in the Wu Dong mountain area of China in the 1920s. As I walked home after class, I began to notice a calm, oceanic feeling. "Step down as if you're stepping on a well of bubbling energy," Ernie would tell us. He said that t'ai chi was a kind of love affair with gravity, and he was right. Every morning, I went through my form, feeling the energy, or chi, moving like slow honey through my bones. Doing the form, I began to understand that I simply couldn't fall off the earth, no matter how much I tried.

T'ai chi is an expression of Taoism, which, depending on what you need, is a religion, a philosophy or a system for good health and longevity. It's based on the Tao, meaning, sort of, the way or flow of the universe. For me, it was a philosophy with overtones of a religion. If you had asked me then, I would have told you that I was a Taoist. Taoism followed that paradoxical way of thinking, the intertwining of opposites that I'd always been comfortable with. Chang Chung-yuan spoke to this view when he described its unity of affirmation and negation:

> In this unity everything breaks though the shell of itself and inter-fuses with every other thing. Each identifies with every other. The one is many and the many is one. In this realm all selves dissolve into one, and all our selves are selves only to the extent that they disappear into all other selves. Each individual merges into every other individual.

I practiced my form for seven years. I studied the Tao De Ching, the book of short verses that form the central text of Taoism. I even calmed down by small degrees. Finally, though, I had to admit that for me, Taoism was more like a dear friend than a lover. I once read a description of the Tao by Holmes Welch that stuck in my mind because it summed up all the pluses and minuses of Taoism:

> To all men [the Tao De Ching] offers a degree of comfort—a cold comfort it is true, not like the comfort of prayer to a merciful God who may, if he chooses, suspend the order of the universe for the sake of a single penitent. Tao can never be suspended. Dark, infinite, and unchanging, it is something a man can depend on to the end of his days. Rationally, intuitively, he can know it, accept it, and bring himself into harmony with it, and mystically he can penetrate to something darker behind it. At each step his comfort will grow, until at last he feels that "mysterious power" which all of us need to feel, confronted by the hostile immensity of the universe. There is little that we cannot face then. It is a wonderful, almost a

miraculous thing that for Lao Tzu this hostile immensity becomes the Mother, symbol of all that is warm and protective.

Yes, I could feel a "mysterious power," but the feeling remained a "cold comfort." Like Buddhism, the Taoism I knew could calm the passions, but that was the problem. It was mild, I was mild, but I still wanted to fall passionately in love. I wanted a true religion, something, someone, I could love with all my heart, mind, and soul.

After eleven years at the agency in New York, I was laid off. The whole economy was in the tank, I couldn't find a job worth the aggravation, so I knocked around Manhattan for a while as a freelancer. That's when Lauren and I decided to move to Austin. Harrison was five, and Lauren was pregnant with Spencer.

Four years went by. We bought a home in the suburbs. The boys were healthy and growing up. Lauren and I were tired, what with the kids, but we knew we were blessed with our quiet, somewhat prosperous, middle-class life. It was all very normal, and that was fine. It takes a lot of work to be normal.

I remember one day when I came home, feeling sorry for myself because of something going on at work, I forget exactly what. I found Spencer on the back veranda, playing with a plastic sword. He told me to kneel in front of him, so I did. Then he tapped me lightly on each shoulder and said in a solemn, little-boy voice, "King Daddy . . ."

I think I have problems, but I don't. Not even close.

And yet, even with a decent job, a wonderful family, a good marriage, why did I feel that my life had been a massive flop? Was I born to go through my days as a suburban dad? Sometimes I would get up at night and wander around the house, just as I'd wandered around my parents' house when I was a teenager, waiting for my life to begin.

I thought about how I had failed as an intellectual. Failed as a scholar. Failed as a writer. After finishing my second book of poems, I had shopped the manuscript around. I couldn't find any takers after a year, so in a fit of pique I self-published it. There were some responses, a few reviews, but I lost my taste for literature, decided to hell with it, boxed up the remaining copies of the book, and stored them in the attic.

Why not? I was just an average person. Average husband, average father, average breadwinner. My whole life was average, but I felt like I was vanishing into the averages.

When I developed diabetes, I began to see myself as old and frail, birdlike. I tried to pray, the way I'd learned in the program, but the prayers wouldn't "take." Even though the diabetes was under control, I was afraid I was going to die. And I wanted to die. I don't mean physical death but dying inside myself, somehow. Twenty years earlier, I had written:

> When I stand at the brilliant edge of the roof,
> There is always the man who continues forward
>
> Without hesitation, slipping smoothly out of my skin
> And I'm lost, watching the back of his head,
>
> His strong arms spreading open as he steps
> Soundlessly over the edge.

I wanted to be that man. I had listened to born-again Christians talking about "falling into Jesus" and I kept trying to hear a call, but nothing happened. I felt impacted, sealed up somehow. It had been years since I'd cried, and that didn't feel healthy. I remember telling Lauren, "We're pikers. Sure, we talk about finding a spiritual path, we read our little paperbacks, and we watch Bill Moyers and Joseph Campbell on PBS, but we're really not committed. We don't have that fire in the belly. We're just fooling around."

A friend in the program once said that he never made life-changing decisions unless his back was against a wall. In a way, that was me. But I can see now that everything I thought was a failure was also a step forward, an invitation and opportunity. Only in a secular sense was I failing. In a truer sense, I was finally being set free.

By the time I reached the abbey, I was primed and ready, more than I realized. God had been silently coaching me for forty-eight years. I was so ready, in fact, that when the right moment came, it took only a tiny push, as if with the tip of his little finger, a push so slight I didn't even notice it, to propel me headlong through an invisible doorway and into a new life.

At the end of the poem "Splittings," Adrienne Rich writes:

> I choose to love this time for once
> with all my intelligence

When I found the church, I felt that something wonderful was happening inside me, and this time I didn't want to screw it up. Every day when I went to Mass, I prayed hard to be able to love this time for once, with all my intelligence.

5

No Divisions

Your words were found, and I ate them, and your words became to me a joy and the delight of my heart.

—Jeremiah 15:16

If you could understand Him, it would not be God.

—St. Augustine

By January I was halfway through the New Testament. I read for two hours every morning, then read in my car in the parking lot during my lunch hour.

I also started reading the Bible as I drove to work, a copy with a soft leather cover so I could balance it on my right knee. Whenever traffic backed up on the freeway or if I came to a red light, I'd look down and read a few lines, maybe from Psalms. I found that I wasn't annoyed anymore with the wait. Waiting was an opportunity, not time stolen out of my life. I also tried to be a Christian driver, patient and courteous, which would have worked fine except for the morons I met on the road who obviously weren't driving with Bibles on their knees.

Along with Scripture I started reading other books: *Christ among Us* by Anthony Wilhelm, *The Book of God* by Gabriel Josipovici, *The Seven Storey Mountain* by Thomas Merton, Richard McBrien's massive *Catholicism*, anthologies from the desert fathers, bits and pieces of *The Imitation of Christ* and *The Cloud of Unknowing*. I read through the Koran, and came away thinking that the arguments among Islam, Judaism, and Christianity were more from similarities than differences.

I read *Amazing Grace* and *The Cloister Walk* by Kathleen Norris, then read her books again.

Each book led to a dozen more. I hadn't been this excited about anything for decades. Learning about Christianity almost from scratch was a colossal task. The marathoner in me was happy.

So was the addict. I knew that I wasn't supposed to focus too much on "spiritual progress." But I wanted to gulp down God, just like I used to drink. I wanted to go faster than my ability to understand, faster than my prayers, faster than Godspeed. I wanted to be already "there," wherever "there" was. Yes, I understood that the path was like Getting Sober; it never ended. But that didn't keep me from wanting to accelerate the process a bit, maybe quiz out of a few areas, do some advanced-placement work before I entered any church.

I wanted a beautifully worn Bible, one frayed around the edges, the pages slightly gray from thousands of turnings. A Bible that showed deep familiarity with God's truth. And I wanted that Bible now.

When I lived in New York, I rode the subway to work every day, and I remember the religious books that the passengers carried. You saw Bibles, Jewish Tanahks and Midrash, the Koran, you name it. I was especially impressed with the African American "church ladies" from Crown Heights. They would get on board, set themselves down, and haul out these huge, black Bibles from their handbags. As they read, they would be underlining almost every verse. With highlighters! Sometimes with ballpoint pens! I was shocked the first time I saw that. Marking up Bibles seemed like, well, a sacrilege. But then I realized that these were *working* Bibles. They were tools, meant to be used and not just examined from a distance. Now I started underlining my own Bible, writing notes in the margins. Every so often, I'd close it and look at the pages sideways to see if it was showing any respectable wear.

I wanted instant wisdom. Partly this was simple ego. How many of us want to be like Christ among the elders, amazing everyone? But I also wanted instant wisdom because I thought it would lead to instant peace of mind. The more I read, the more I felt rattled and exposed. The open-heart surgery that I'd felt when I began going to Mass kept getting deeper and wouldn't stop. Something was breaking up inside me. I looked at the essay by Clarissa Pinkola Estés in *Goddess of the Americas*:

> There is great power in the broken heart. Unlike many aspects of psyche that might close or hide when hurt, the heart broken open stays open. Though painful for certain, the heart broken open can be a blessing beyond compare.

I still prayed to God to break open my heart, but underneath I was getting scared, and the more I read, the more I wanted to hide inside my reading. By February I was in a bind. Should I be reading less? More? Was I finding God or just turning into a Bible junkie, a church geek, chasing after one spiritual high after another?

One morning I closed my eyes and asked, "Jesus, what should I do?" I saw him holding me up. I saw myself as a skinny, middle-aged man out of breath. His arms were strong, and he held my face in front of his. Then the image went away.

The next day, I looked up from my reading and asked him again, "What should I do?" I saw him standing in front of me, very calm, with his arms open.

"Believe in me," he said, very simply, without any inflection. Was that a command? A statement? Even a question?

"I do believe in you," I said out loud. "I believe." I listened to myself. Was I just talking to myself at the kitchen table? Had Jesus really said something to me? And if he had, what did he mean? What did belief really mean?

I kept listening, but I didn't hear anything more.

"I believe in you." I kept repeating those words, day after day, like batting practice, swinging the bat until you can do it from inside your
body without thinking, without hesitating. Fake It Till You Make It.

But what did belief really mean? A beautifully worn Bible wasn't
like buying prewashed jeans. You earned that wear. The church ladies'
Bibles were beat up from being carried to work every day and to
church and study groups year after year. Those Bibles were read in
kitchens and bedrooms, in bathrooms if that was the only quiet place
they could find. They represented faith as a way of life, an attempt,
if nothing else, to be an honest Christian in an indifferent, even hostile, world. I realized that one of the reasons I was reading so fast was
that it gave me the illusion of understanding more than I did. If I
slowed down and asked myself what those words really meant, how
they applied to our lives, I couldn't say.

Somebody once told me in the program that the mark of spiritual
progress isn't in what you feel or think or know. It's in what you do. I
couldn't be a solitary student, or a desert saint sitting on a pillar. I had
to carry my baby faith into the world. In *Christ among Us*, one of the
study questions asks what you'd say if you had to put all of Christianity
on a bumper sticker. I decided mine would say "No Divisions." That
was the message of Christ, I thought. We can't have artificial divisions
in our lives, us against them, neighbor against neighbor, us against
God, even us against parts of ourselves that we want to despise or glo-
rify. No compartments, no walls, no divisions. I think that was what
drove Jesus nuts about the Pharisees: they tried to maintain, with the
best of intentions, divisions between those who observed the law and
those who didn't. Even their name meant those who are apart. So that
was belief: carrying my faith into the world, loving publicly as a Christian, with no divisions.

Oh great. I'm a bookish introvert. That was the last thing I wanted to do. But that was precisely why I had to do it. An old friend, the one who brought me into the program, once told me that she had entered the program herself after reading Meister Eckhart. Somewhere he says that making spiritual progress is easy. All you have to do is find the single hardest thing for you to do—and then do that thing. For her at the time, it was giving up alcohol. For me, it would be more than reading or sticking a fish symbol on my Subaru. It would be coming out of my nook and living as a Christian with my wife, my kids, and everyone at work.

So let's start with work. Let's see if I can talk about my boss and still sound Christian.

I had started a new job at a web design start-up. In fact, I began only three days after I came back from the monastery. Every morning I would read and pray, have my spiritual crisis for the day, then take a shower, eat breakfast, and race off to work. I was the marketing communications guy, and I reported to the CEO, a woman I'll simply call the Boss. I won't tell you her real name because she still scares the hell out of me.

She's a New England WASP, a tall, broad-shouldered woman (rowed crew for MIT) with blonde hair raked back so tight it makes her cheekbones shiny. When I worked with her, she was a machine. She would put in a twelve-hour day, then go to the gym downstairs and lift extremely big weights for an hour just to relax, then return for another three or four hours in front of the computer. She lived for work and seemed lost without it. Sometimes I'd go into the office on Saturday mornings, and she was always there, bouncing around the empty hallways like a BB in a tin can.

As CEO, she did everything except the laundry. She spearheaded sales, wrote every project proposal herself (usually after hours), schmoozed the clients, attended the trade shows, and mapped out marketing strategy—all in addition to riding herd on expenses, remodeling the hallways, hiring new employees, and ordering coffee for the kitchenette. On any given day, it seemed that she carried the entire company on her shoulders, determined but seething at the incompetence she saw all around her.

To be honest, she was always more than the caricature I sometimes wanted her to be. When employees brought their children to visit the office, she was delighted, playing with them on the carpet in her office. She was also a demon gardener, and she sometimes talked about the pleasures of digging in the dirt, the smell of fresh earth, and the peaceful feeling she got from dragging bags of mulch up and down the hillside where she lived.

I also reminded myself that like all of us, she had her issues. Her mother was a corporate comptroller who played cello in a symphony and ran the Boston marathon every spring. Her father, an industrialist, spent most of his time at board meetings and could never remember the ages of his children. The Boss also had to deal with the usual challenges of making her way in a male-dominated business world. What's more, she was only thirty-two and still learning about business itself, management, people, and life in general. Only a few years back she'd been a student in business school. Even though she was almost six feet tall, she wore boots with high heels and worried constantly about being taken seriously. This was odd, because we all took her seriously. We knew that we'd better.

When I first interviewed with her, I thought *Classification: Difficult Person.* She reminded me of certain women in my family, very tense and controlling. Maybe for that reason, I thought I could handle her. She'd been cordial enough during the interviews and accommodating when we talked about compensation and title, but from the first day, I was working for a martinet. If I said something, she stepped on my sentence. If I made a suggestion, she dismissed it with a slight, irritated wave of her hand. I felt like an idiot. I was saying yes ma'am to this person young enough—depressing thought—to be my daughter. "I've forgotten more about marketing communications than you'll ever know," I yelled at her, mentally. I reminded myself that I'd been in business for twenty years instead of her measly four. The only consolation was that she treated everyone the same way. I saw others coming out of her office looking whipped and discouraged. I imagined her as a military officer, inspecting the troops every morning, barking orders, whacking a riding crop against her jodhpurs.

The job was a test in humility and trust. I barely made passing grades. For the first few months, while I was getting up at four-thirty, I was also rewriting the entire website for the company and going through all the usual stress and rigamarole of a new job, trying to reassure the Boss that she hadn't made a colossal mistake in hiring me. I worked through the Christmas holiday. I worked New Year's Eve and New Year's Day. I worked six days a week through January. Every now and then, I would see the Boss stalking down the hallway, seething about revenue or the price of brochures or a client she thought was trying to take advantage of her. She said very little to me.

Finally we rolled out the new site late one Saturday night. She looked it over for a minute, uttered the word *Good*, and then went back upstairs to work on a new sales proposal.

I was crushed. I can go for miles on a single word of praise, but I need that encouraging nod every now and then. I told myself that maybe she just didn't know how she came across to others. Besides, who was I being the critic? What had I been doing at her age? Working at a liquor store and trying to write three lines of verse. She was running a ten-million-dollar company, a company that paid its bills on time and supported more than two hundred people. How could I look down my nose at that? Who did I think I was, just because I read the Bible every day?

Nevertheless, every day was a challenge. I would walk across the parking lot in the morning quoting the Psalms. "Lord, protect me from my enemies." The office wasn't cutthroat. I worked with decent people. But I couldn't bring myself to trust the situation.

Things continued to get worse. I remember one day when I was working late at the office. My hands were shaking as I typed because the Boss had told me that I didn't "have my head in the game" (she loved sports metaphors), that the proposal needed to be finished by 8:00 a.m. or else. "If I don't manage every step, nothing gets accomplished around here!" she said.

That's a damn lie! I thought. Well, okay, maybe there was some grain of truth there. Maybe I could be working harder. I'd been taking long lunches, going to Mass at St. Edward's. I'd been getting to the office at nine instead of at dawn when she arrived. But as I typed, I was still angry, yelling, screaming at her in my head. "Totally unfair! Sure I can always do more, but I don't drop the ball. I don't screw up. Give me a deadline and I'll hit it. And if you did your job better, you'd know what a sweet deal you have with me!"

I finished up around eight, still furious, adrenaline pumping. As I walked out to my car, feeling sorry for myself, I said to Jesus, "Here, take my anger." I gave him a dark ball of black thorns. Almost immediately I felt the anger leaving me. I stood there for a minute under the trees, listening to the crickets, amazed.

I got in my car and shut my eyes. I asked, "What do you do with all the anger that people give you?"

He gave me a slight, brief smile and said simply, *I love it,* meaning, I think, that he loved the anger until it went away. And it did in my case, for that day at least.

Wallace Stevens carried a briefcase divided into two parts. On one side he kept the papers from the insurance company where he worked as a vice president. On the other were his poetry manuscripts. He was proud, maybe even amused at the neat division. For years I'd been maintaining the same divisions in my life, living as the Secret Poet in the business world. I'd wasted a good part of my life resenting the fact that I had to fit my inner life behind a day job. But No Divisions meant that I couldn't barricade myself against my job anymore. I'd have to learn to work with the Boss and even—hard as it was—to pray for her and for the company.

I also had to own the fact that the Boss irritated me precisely because we were so alike. We both took ourselves way too seriously, and we both bristled when criticized. We were also both introverts trying to adapt to a business world that is basically ruled by extroverts. She was trying to fit the world into neat boxes on a spreadsheet, just as I had with stanzas of poetry. She once criticized me for not getting out and schmoozing enough with the local business community, but she also kept to herself, all things considered. Many times I'd pass her office and see her in there with the lights off, perched behind her massive executive desk and peering into the glow of the computer monitor, typing and tinkering for hours, and I recognized that distant expression on her face, at peace in her private world.

My own private world at home was centered in an extra bedroom next to the garage, set apart from the daily traffic and kid noise of the house. It was intended as a study when we built the house. I had this Edwardian idea in my mind—"Father is in the study, thinking deep thoughts"—so I painted the walls a deep baronial red, and Lauren found some red leather chairs at a garage sale. I used it as my mini-monastery where I read every morning while the family was still asleep. It was my favorite time of the day. No problems. No issues. Just the calm and simple happiness of learning more about what you love.

When I emerged, blinking, every day for breakfast, I always found that life, oddly enough, was still happening. Harrison, our elder son, was having more problems at school. He was in the third grade, and the teachers sent him to detention several times a week. Lauren talked to counselors almost daily. Harrison's teachers said he was bright but unfocused. Nothing happened, they said, unless they managed him every step of the way.

Like both parents, Harrison lives very much in his head. In the morning I'd tell him to brush his teeth, then find him ten minutes later still in the bathroom, holding a toothbrush slack in his mouth, staring off at some invisible horizon in the mirror, swaying slightly on one foot. "FOCUS! FOCUS! FOCUS!" I'd yell. "Nothing happens unless I nag you constantly! You've got to learn to focus!"

I was wasting my breath. I once gave him a lecture over the phone about something I can't even remember. Afterward, Lauren asked him what I'd been talking about, and he said, "I don't know. It was just one long string of Chinese."

For a while, his teachers strongly hinted about using Ritalin, thinking he had attention deficit disorder. I wondered if I had been the same way at that age, but like many parents I remember myself only as a dutiful little worker, which I might have been. But maybe Harrison's dreaminess infuriated me because I had squashed the dreamer inside myself. I was working long hours, and I hated my job. Each day I had to bite my lip and hunker down and endure the grind, and so, by God, would he.

Was this the big lesson about life I was trying to teach him? That life was a disappointment, that work was a pain and constant frustration? Inside, I was dazzled every day with what I was learning about

God and Catholicism, but was I showing it in my life, in the way I loved him? If the boys learned only from what I did, not from what I said, then what in God's name was I teaching them?

Both our kids were prayed-for children, and I knew that along with Lauren, the boys were the biggest blessings I'd ever received in my life. But you couldn't tell that from the way I acted. I wanted the Christian life? No Divisions? Well, here was my chance, here was my duty. Harrison had once drawn a picture of himself as a boy in a little boat on a stormy sea. Overhead, guiding the boat, was a beam of light from a lighthouse on the shore. I pointed to a stick figure on top of the lighthouse. "Who's this guy?"

"That's you," he said.

Oh dear Lord. Blessed is the dad who can be the lighthouse keeper for his children. Each day I tried to remember that here was another chance to share what I was learning. In the middle of tantrums and arguments and bottoms that needed wiping, I kept thinking, *Jesus, Jesus, help me remember your word.* And when I forgot, which was all the time, I tried to remember that each day was also a chance to learn from my kids. One evening I showed Harrison a cartoon from the *New Yorker:* An enormous father in a white shirt and tie is looking down at a worried-looking little boy who's perched on his knee. The father is saying "Let's have a heart-to-heart talk—one huge, powerful grown-up to one tiny, nothing kid."

"Is that how you sometimes feel?" I asked. Later I noticed that he'd cut the cartoon out and tacked it to his bulletin board.

⚮

One day, Lauren said, "You look a lot better since you started praying. You're letting go, not holding on to the tree stump. You're letting the current take you along." She seemed to be happy for me, buying me little Catholic gifts from time to time, little postcards or pictures of Our Lady. She understood the culture.

I could see that something was happening with her as well, though I didn't know what. For years she'd been reading New Age books. She gave psychic readings, and she had some sort of ability in her hands to calm and sometimes even heal. I could feel it myself. She would rub her palms together and slowly move her hands around me, and I had a feeling like silk that flowed down through my body and gave me a very real, physical sense of peace.

Around February she started reading the *Conversations with God* series of books by Neale Donald Walsch. Every night, in the few minutes we had between getting the boys to sleep and going to sleep ourselves, we would read in bed, and I would hear her yellow highlighter squeaking across the page, a few words, then several lines, then every paragraph, just like the "church ladies" in New York. I could feel her thinking, *Yes! Yes! Yes!!!* Finally, I couldn't concentrate and put my own book down and said, "Why don't you just underline the whole damn book?"

She looked at me, surprised. I was surprised at myself. Why was I getting so upset? Maybe because I could feel her enthusiasm and it didn't exactly feel Catholic.

She'd been trying to find something to believe in for years, just as I had. In fact, she told me that her wandering began when—me and my big mouth—I told her I wasn't a Christian. That started her thinking, she said, and introduced her to the idea that maybe you could be something other than a daughter of the church. Up to that time, she'd been going to Mass every day at noon.

A few weeks later she began reading *When God Was a Woman* by Merlin Stone. That was at the beginning of feminist theology, and then she was off and running, reading hundreds of what New Agers called "metaphysical" books about spirituality, reincarnation, auras, the causal plane, and so on. She went through a tarot period. She gave readings. She talked about seeing auras. She read about near-death experiences and past-life regressions, during which you go back through your past lives to uncover traumas or unresolved issues.

At the time, she seemed to have it all thought out. She explained that we were "God experiencing," that our lives were how God learned about the physical world. It was a kind of nonjudgmental process theology. Once in the East Village in New York, she said, "God doesn't care," and that phrase stuck in my mind. The thought seemed liberating and Zenlike in its acceptance of the *thingness* of things. She didn't mean that God was indifferent but that he was all-accepting. She was working toward a sense of the divine as supremely nonjudgmental, like Brahma, an impersonal, almost indifferent force like pure energy. Perhaps she was attracted to this notion because her own upbringing had been so judgmental. If she wanted to swing all the way from a vertical, hierarchical, and transcendent view of God to something that was completely horizontal and immanent, that was fine with me. The way she looked at God and the universe could be quite beautiful. She often talked about the human race as billions of tiny souls floating through the universe like galaxies, rising and falling, life after life, and the poet in me appreciated the image.

Besides, what did I know back then? Like some men, I wasn't particularly confident when it came to religion. Faith was a woman thing, and I once asked her, truly mystified, how she could believe in God.

"It's like when you're a child," she said. "You know that deep down, you're surrounded by love, that your parents totally, absolutely love you, regardless of what happens day to day. I had that feeling growing up, so that's why I can believe."

Perhaps her home life wasn't the horror show she sometimes painted, I thought. Anyway, for sixteen years we rocked along. We both kept reading, talking, trying to understand. But we were both dissatisfied.

But now, this year after the monastery, I was locked into a tractor beam. I was focused, and I realized that now I had to make choices. When I saw Lauren reading *Conversations with God*, my ears pricked up. I wanted both of us to be on a path of discovery, but I also wanted her path to be just like mine. I honestly believed, and still do, that I'd found the way, the truth, and the life.

I was also being a classic convert. Converts want the whole world not only to convert but also to convert the way they have. I once had a writer friend in Minneapolis who was as self-contained as I was. Then he discovered psychoanalysis. After his first session he cried nonstop for three days. After that, he went around to all his friends, especially the guys, telling them that they should get in touch with their feelings and go into analysis, just like him. I wanted to pinch his head off. Now here I was, acting the same way. Forget the fact that six months ago I thought Christianity was for dummies.

And let's be honest: I also wanted to be the star in the family. We're talking gross ego. Dad was finding God, and that was more important than what anyone else believed, right? I wanted to be this big ball of illumination, leading my grateful wife and kids back to the One True Church. In my secret fantasy we were going to be a Catholic poster family, happily going to Mass every Sunday. We would pray together, stay together, and say the rosary together, with everyone finding a new life in Christ. Just like me.

⚮

The morning after I groused at Lauren for underlining everything in *Conversations with God*, I apologized and asked, "So, what's the big deal? What's it about?"

"It's just one of my books you keep turning your nose up at."

"You think I should read it?"

"No, and I won't show it to you. It talks about God but it doesn't talk about church, or any church for that matter. Really sweetie, I just don't think you're ready to handle it." And that's all she said.

Naturally I sneaked a look the next few days. Admittedly I only glanced at the book. That first year, I was in such a newborn and fragile state, I handled with tongs anything that was even remotely non-Catholic. I avoided many people, places, and things because I didn't feel strong enough to defend my baby faith, and I was constantly afraid of losing it. I didn't read anything about the historical Jesus, for example, because I was afraid that I might slip into a secular view of thinking he was just another highly effective motivational speaker and charismatic healer. When I looked at the *Conversations with God* book, I read enough to get upset, although it was just your basic New Age theology: "There are no 'shoulds' or 'shouldn'ts' in God's world. Do what you want to do. Do what reflects you, what represents you as a grander version of your Self."

The book was your basic horizontal immanent theology taken to the extreme.

Walsch's books—he wrote two more in quick succession— obviously spoke to many people who were dissatisfied or repelled by the Gospels and Christian churches, not to mention Catholicism. I flipped through the pages, looking at passages Lauren had highlighted and underlined, with big stars drawn in the margins and exclamation points. The book talked about fear and how evil was only fear that we haven't yet recognized and tamed. How much fear did she have in her heart, and how much of that fear was Catholic born?

A few weeks went by. I wondered if maybe she just had a problem with groups. She once told me a story about a friend who worked as an American Communist organizer in Detroit. She told her mother about her friend and how idealistic the party seemed to be. Lauren added that she was actually thinking about joining the Communist Party herself. Her mother just laughed and said, "Oh Laurie, you didn't even join the Girl Scouts." Her mom was right. Lauren wasn't a joiner. She had always had major problems working for any group, any corporation, and the church was one of the largest corporate bodies in the world.

When I talked about me and the boys joining the church, hinting that Lauren might rejoin with us, she told me, "You like labyrinths. You like working in corporations. But I need space. You prefer to worship in a labyrinth, and the church is a wonderfully deep and complicated labyrinth for you. I need to worship in open fields."

Still, she seemed supportive. She helped me get the kids to church every Sunday and talked with me about what I was reading. One evening I told her about talking to a nun at a local church about a Catholic initiation program called the Rite of Christian Initiation of Adults. Lauren seemed interested enough, so I chatted away, telling her that the nun said it was an enriching experience for couples to go through together, especially if one had been born into the church. That way, the cradle Catholic could sponsor the initiate and—

She blew up. "Look, I'll support you, and I'll do whatever I can to help you right now," she said, her voice rising. "For you, the Catholic Church is perfect. It's something you've been looking for all your life. But don't ask me to walk the same path! If you haven't noticed, I've been moving away from the church for years. And just when you fell in love with her, I also discovered something new. I don't know what it is yet. But it's not Catholic, that's for sure. It's not even Christian. I'm not asking you to join me. Just respect my own path."

I felt as if she'd slapped me, as if she had told me she was having an affair. I felt panic. "Don't leave me! I can't go through this alone!" I wanted to say. Instead I said, "The church is like a two-hundred-lane highway. There's room for almost everyone. That is why they call it Catholic. It's universal."

"Listen to me," she said.

"I'm listening! I'm listening!"

"No you're not." She paused, then said, "The church is great for you but not for me. I can't even begin to tell you what I'm thinking these days."

"Why not?"

"Because I love you! You're tender right now, and you're not ready to hear it."

At this point, Spencer burst into the bedroom crying, with Harrison following him and denying everything. We got the boys back into bed, then went to bed ourselves. I was still bewildered, but by now I was also mad. Stiff-necked woman! *Who do you think you are, you and your Hollywood theologians!!* I didn't say anything though. Neither did Lauren. We turned out the lights. After a few moments, our hands found each other in the dark. We patted each other, but there were still hard feelings on both sides as we fell asleep.

The next morning I got up and sat down to read at the kitchen table. I paused for a moment and asked, "Okay, Jesus, what do I do about Lauren?"

Then I heard, very distinctly and without emotion, *Don't tell her what to think.* I asked for more, but that's all I heard, so that's what I did.

After we had a sudden argument one evening about the Trinity—

"It's clumsy and artificial! No wonder so many books have to be written about it!"

"Who are you to judge two thousand years of theology!"

—we decided to put an embargo on theological discussions after eight in the evening. Then we extended the embargo to weeknights as well. Then we stopped talking about God and church altogether. I thought of two thunderheads on a summer night. Occasionally there were flashes of heat lightning and the rumble of thunder in the distance. She read her books. I read mine.

Our Baptist friends didn't say much, but I could feel them quietly gauging whether my wife was going to hell. "It's all in the Bible," they told me. "I am the way, the truth, and the life." I chewed on that quite a bit. It seemed right to believe that there were many paths to God, but Lauren put that notion to the test. She wanted to find her own path; she wasn't a joiner, but that's what worried me. I agreed with Wilhelm in *Christ among Us*: "We surely cannot find God only in isolation; it is too easy to come up with a magnified version of our own ego."

On her side, Lauren was finding that there were many people, almost all of them women, who had backed away from Christianity. We have a friend in Santa Fe who was raised Catholic, from an Italian family, but she left the church years ago. Lauren told her about my stay with the monks and my plans to join the church. "Ooooh," the friend said ominously. "They got him."

At least Lauren would keep me from forgetting that all the world wasn't Catholic, not that I wanted to be reminded. Besides, we were still very married to each other. One day, setting up some files in my office, I ran across an old postcard that she had sent me when we were first together. It was an Edward Hopper painting, a woman sitting at a café table, the night behind her, looking away, full of thought, lovely and lonely. "I'd be lost without you," she had written in her beautiful hand. I put the card away in a safe place for all the usual reasons and also because I knew clearly that I'd be lost without her as well.

I was still chanting my way through the Bible, finishing up the history books, but I was getting weary. Second Maccabees almost broke me. Both books of Maccabees seemed—this was my fatigue talking—more history than the revealed word. I slogged through the letters of this and that group making their case to this and that government. It all felt flat and secular, like reading the six-o'clock news. I sighed, thinking how far we'd come from those amazing stories in Genesis where every detail glowed with significance. I slogged on, but I kept getting colds, and then my ears stopped up. "Maybe you don't want to hear something," said Lauren.

She might have been right. I was still on the road, still the long-distance runner. Nike once had a poster that showed a country lane and in the distance the little figure of a runner. The headline said, "There Are No Finish Lines." This was the same feeling. I was starting a process that would last the rest of my life and beyond. At the same time, I was exhausted.

One Sunday, we went to Mass at St. Catherine's. Afterward we talked to Father Dick about joining the parish. Father was a massive, gentle man, well over two hundred pounds. He looked you very directly in the eye, but he had a calming, very reassuring manner. I had seen him walking through the congregation before Mass, chatting with the members, working the crowd like a good pastor. He stopped by a young couple with a crying baby. He smiled and asked for the baby and held it in his arms. In a few seconds, the baby settled down and stopped crying altogether and fell asleep.

Father Dick told us about St. Catherine's, and we promised to come back. Later at home, Lauren and I talked about our conversation, and she mentioned that I seemed very small standing next to Father Dick. "Well, the guy's big as a bear!" I said. "Anybody would seem small next to him!"

"I know. But besides that."

"Maybe I'm just not driven." I was asking a lot of questions about myself in those days.

"I hope not. People who are driven have something missing. You just seemed . . . well, small."

Lauren is my truth teller. She was right. When I stopped drinking in New York and entered the program, I felt small at first and reduced. I felt the same way now. One morning a few days before, I had seen an image, half dream and half daydream, where some sort of shrub or bush was rooting down through my body and growing up through my torso and shooting out the top, expanding and growing thicker until I was crowned with a large semicircle of branches over my head. It was an image of growth and abundance, but it unnerved me because the larger the bush grew, the less I became until finally I was just a thin sheath for this massive growth moving up through my body.

But that's the point, right? More God, less me? I remembered in G. B. Shaw's *Major Barbara* where a character says, "You have learnt something. That always feels at first as if you had lost something." And I thought of the Taoists who said that the wise man's library always gets smaller but the foolish scholar is always collecting more books. (My own bookcase was filling up nicely.) I had always liked the idea of trading knowledge for wisdom, being able to reduce all the information I was gathering to a simple but deep wisdom. The very idea gave me a sort of wistful, heroic feeling. But I wasn't feeling wise these days. Just small and kind of beat up.

That night after visiting St. Catherine's, I asked Lauren to give me a reading. When she read for people, she would hold an object belonging to the person, something personal that had soaked up their energy, and say whatever came into her head. Was that a bunch of hooey? I didn't know. I was trying to listen to God in the same way, saying what came into my head.

I gave her an old T-shirt, and she held it for a long time, several minutes, and shuddered once. It seemed like she was watching a movie. Then she said, "I see you as a tiny, tiny figure with outstretched arms lifted slightly, and somebody, something, tells me that you've found a gateway, some sort of path to no-self. And then you're growing smaller and smaller until there's only a song left. You've disappeared. No words finally. Just singing."

Then she said, "I see us traveling when we're very old. Much bowing. I see this thin, gaunt old man. Is that you? Well, the voice says yes, sort of. Very old, very bent over."

I finally finished Maccabees, and moved to the Wisdom Books. Then one morning, as I sat in the parking lot at work, preparing to face the Boss for another day, I suddenly had a thought: *If I become a Christian, I'm going to have to die.*

Well, of course. Years ago, I'd written in a journal: "Jesus says: Come to me and die." That was Christ to me, someone asking for sacrifice. Maybe that had kept me away from him, a sense that I'd have to die to myself, to the false self that keeps us away from God. No wonder I'd never been enthusiastic. I had cozied up to self-destruction for years, but this was different. I wasn't looking for oblivion or melodrama this time. I was looking for more life, not less.

Here was the final meaning of No Divisions: the death of the self that stands between ourselves and God. The next morning, feeling strange, I shut my eyes and said, "Jesus, I want to die."

Of course you want to die. And you want to live. Live through me. He took my face in his hands and looked me straight in the eyes. Then he said very slowly and distinctly, as if explaining something about traf-

fic safety to a little child who doesn't yet understand, *You can die*. . .
through me . . . and still live.

That was all. I was running on a road, and I didn't know where I was going. I just knew that I couldn't go back; I had to move forward. And I knew that I couldn't do it by myself.

6

Among the Episcopalians

Somehow the word got out in the neighborhood that the Coles were unchurched and shopping around. The Baptist family on the corner started dropping hints, and a few fundamentalist neighbors extended their carefully worded invitations. Nobody tried to muscle us into the fold, but I could feel us being watched.

One night, Martin, our neighbor down the street, stopped by. Our boys played together, and he was returning one of Spencer's superhero toys. I'd been talking with him on and off about churchgoing, and he had told me about his own community, a small Presbyterian group that had splintered off another group from Dallas. They seemed conservative. When he came by, I asked him inside, but he stayed outside, hovering on the porch. He would never come inside our house. Maybe he spotted the Hindu statues in our front hallway.

He invited me to his church once more. I told him we were thinking of an Episcopalian church in north Austin, but we were still going around to various churches, trying to see what fit. "We're just following our heart!" I said, a bit gaily, trying to sound like Joseph Campbell.

"Oh, no. No" he said, "You don't want to do that. Read Matthew 15:19: 'From the heart come evil thoughts, murder, adultery, unchastity, theft, false witness, blasphemy.'"

Damn. My first Christian faux pas. What could I say? He was quoting Jesus. At the same time, I was irritated about being embarrassed. *Of course you trust your heart!* I thought. *Why not?*

He continued. "There are three things you need when you select a church. Number one, correct doctrine, because that's the foundation of everything else. Second, support and proper relations between you and the community in dealing with one other and in dealing as a group with the world. Third, discipline."

He stood in the darkness outside, swaying slightly. I think he was shy talking about this. A part of me wanted to turn the porch light on for him, but a part of me didn't. I really didn't know what to do. I couldn't think of a biblical quote to quote back, so I said a few nebulous things and thanked him for the toy. He invited me once more to visit his church. I thanked him, and he left.

The next morning I was still upset. My pride had been injured. Here I was, reading the Bible every day for months, and I hadn't thought of a single comeback. Obviously I wasn't ready for dueling verses. Later I would understand a bit more about Presbyterian theology, about John Knox and John Calvin. About double predestination and the belief that some of us are saved, others damned, and there's ultimately nothing you can do.

Part of me was intrigued with the absoluteness of that theology. It seemed almost Islamic, a total and complete surrender to the will of an all-controlling God. But at the same time, I was disturbed, partly because the theology seemed dark, but partly because his group represented something uncontrolled, almost anarchic about the Protestant world. It was the idea that if you didn't like your church, you just pulled up stakes and formed another one. I could see the appeal. It was like a hi-tech start-up where everything is fresh and exciting and everyone has six jobs and works day and night, and belongs to this tight little family trying to make it happen. But working in start-ups can be isolating, and it's easy to go off in bizarre directions because the sum total of everyone's knowledge in the company is still fairly small. Big corporations can be ponderous and oppressive, but they've also made enough mistakes and they're old enough to know what works and what doesn't. Besides, at the end of the Protestant splintering process, you just have splinters, smaller and smaller splinters evolving toward the ultimate splinter: a church of one. I wanted to join a church, or at least a denomination, that was larger, way larger, than myself.

We started going to an Episcopal church every Sunday with the boys. It was a modest little community with a great playground. The boys liked the small chapel and the doughnuts afterwards. Lauren and I appreciated the sermons by Father Norm. He was a solidly built man who could have been the branch manager at a bank. He was married with a grown daughter, and his wife worked in the children's educational programs.

"This could be a kind of starter church for us," Lauren said. The community had only a couple hundred members. Everyone was friendly in a small-town sort of way, although I felt that, like a small town, you'd have to be a member for quite a while before you really fit.

I had no basic disputes with the theology, and the Mass was largely Catholic in form, though I thought I noticed a few differences. They offered the Host with all due respect, but—maybe it was my imagination—they seemed to be just a teeny bit casual in the way they treated it. To Catholics, the consecrated Host was the literal body of Christ, not just a symbol, and the priests handled it like plutonium. Not a single molecule was left untended. As a whole, however, the Episcopalian Mass seemed Catholic enough. At communion, we'd all kneel together at the altar rail: me, Lauren, and Harrison receiving the Host and the wine, Spencer receiving a blessing.

Looking back, I think that a larger church might have been too overwhelming for us. I compared faith communities to those moving sidewalks you see at airports. They helped you proceed a bit faster than you could walking by yourself. For us, our little church was moving at just the right speed. Any faster and we might have been knocked off our feet. That church was where I first started telling my story, a bit at a time. I talked about coming back from the monastery and being on a path, and everyone nodded; they understood. And as I talked about where I'd been, I gradually began to see where I needed to go.

I kept going to Mass, of course. On Sundays I'd catch an early Mass somewhere, then swing by the house, pick up my family and take them to the Episcopal church.

During the week I sometimes went to 5:45 Mass at San José's. I'd walk past the Boss's office door, trying not to be noticed. She was still at it, her head down. Just getting her second wind, actually. I could feel her look up and frown as I sneaked out the door.

One evening after Mass I was wandering around the church, and I discovered something called a Chapel of Perpetual Adoration. When I first walked in, the place seemed dark and creepy. All my Protestant feelers were twitching. The air was stale and sweet with an odd smell, either incense or cheap disinfectant. Three or four people were seated in the little pews, some praying, some just sitting. In the front, there was a silver cross with a disk in the middle, which I later learned was the Eucharistic Host. A young woman wearing a scarf looked up at me, then returned to her reading. An old air conditioner was working hard in the background, kicking on for a few minutes, then kicking off.

I looked around and discovered a sign-in log beside the door. And then I understood what was going on. People were praying in this chapel, in front of the consecrated Host, but doing this around the clock! Day and night, seven days a week, twenty-four hours a day! I looked through the log. Sure enough, there were names for every slot. Venancio was signed up for 2:00 to 3:00 a.m. on Tuesdays and Thursdays. Lucille checked in at 6:00 a.m. every day for an hour, Maria at 7:00 a.m. I was astonished and fascinated. It was a window into a part of Catholic devotion that I'd heard about but never seen before. I said to myself, *Toto, we're not in Kansas anymore.*

I stayed a few minutes longer, but I couldn't breathe in there. I needed fresh air. At home I told Lauren what I'd seen. Oh yeah, she knew all about Perpetual Adoration. "You'll be there someday, taking a shift," she said.

That night I kept thinking about the chapel. All night long there would be someone there, praying, maybe just sitting, but keeping watch. Like a power utility, it never closed, never shut down. Each person stayed until the next person showed up.

The next time I visited San José, I went straight to the chapel. Outside I read a bit about adoration: neighborhoods where this occurs have lower crime rates, etc., etc.

I opened the door. The minute I stepped inside, I was almost overwhelmed with the impulse to throw myself down on the carpet in front of the host. Suddenly the whole idea of devotion to the Eucharist made all the sense in the world. This chapel was holy. On the wall I noticed a small, handwritten notice: "Do Not Lie on the Floor."

I was slowly making progress through the Old Testament. I wanted to thrash through the pages like a Massey Ferguson combine, leaving neat rows of underlined verses behind me as I gathered up worlds of incredible wisdom and insight every morning. Instead, I was aware of how little I was remembering, or even understanding, as I chanted along. I had read through all of Shakespeare in grad school, and that gave me at least a general sense of what he had to say. The same with James Joyce or William Carlos Williams. But I couldn't get my arms around the Bible. It was the hardest book I'd ever tried to read. All I could do was get a sense of the lay of the land, which way was north as I wandered along, and that didn't seem to be near enough. It was one thing to read the deep-image poets and blithely appreciate what I couldn't understand. But this was about God and my immortal soul. This was crucial. There might be a test at the end.

I trudged through Psalms and Proverbs, taking notes and writing outlines. The student in me wanted to master this book, but it wasn't a book, it was a library. I tried to slow down. I knew I was going faster than my prayers, going at the speed of ego. I thought of Bonhoeffer's phrase: "ungodly haste." I thought of Thomas Merton's warning that busyness is a form of violence.

One morning before dawn I was sitting on the back veranda with my coffee mug. I closed my eyes and saw Jesus holding me up again. *Love me*, he said, and again, insistent. *Love me!*

"But I do!"

No, you don't. You slap me away, withdraw into your little corner. I want you to go slower. Then even slower until you stop. And when you finally stop, there I'll be, loving you. But you have to stop. Right now, you're passing over my love.

I thought of something Lauren had told me years ago when Harrison was a toddler. We were both new parents, riddled with fatigue, but I probably seemed especially oblivious to the one-year-old at my feet as I pecked away at the keyboard every weekend. "Appreciate your son!" Lauren said, trying to break into my shell. "He's never going to be a baby again! These are sacred times!"

These also were sacred times. What was I failing to notice now?

I tried to slow down, at least to stop drinking coffee (so much). The first morning I felt gray and fragmented, but I began to wonder whether these predawn sessions with the Bible and too much coffee were the clearest moments of the day or the most distorted. Was I searching for God or just a more potent, concentrated sense of my own identity?

I tried reading less, praying more, and praying that was more listening and watching than anything else. I found myself thinking about why I had ever been a writer and whether I would write again. Other than journals and commercial work, I hadn't written anything for years, so I thought, why not? I'll be shameless. I'll ask Jesus whether I would ever write six lines that could make me immortal.

I'm disappointed at the question. Soften your heart. Then he left.

I turned to Our Lady, the Blessed Virgin Mary, and asked her the same question. I heard, *You wanted poems that didn't violate the rest of your life or who you were. That's why they were only so big and no bigger. You can't chase after success or even beauty. You must open your heart to the enormous, ugly—do you know what that means?—and glorious Holy Spirit, like I did. Adore, respect the rushing Spirit. Don't follow what you want to see but what the Spirit wants you to see.*

I felt that I should look inside myself, so I did. I saw something that seemed like egg sacs, dull brown and leathery, still unbroken.

I waited a few days. Then one last time I asked Jesus, "Can I write poems or even brochures, anything at all, and do it in your name?"

You can describe your own limits. You can talk about your helpless condition. You can describe your own lack of faith and your distance from God. You can do all that, as much as you want. But you can't describe loving me. Not yet, because you don't. You love yourself and your own fear of annihilation. And yes, you will be annihilated if you never love me. Drop your fears, all of them, every single one, and I will be your name.

Incline your ear, and come to me; listen, so that you may live.
                                        —Isaiah 55:3

Trying to calm down, I spent more time sitting on the back veranda steps in the morning, hearing what I could hear. A breeze would move through trees. *That's God,* I thought. Clouds floating across the sky, or leaves scattered across the street. That was God's handwriting, his signature.

In South America there's the saying that bread is the face of God, and I tried to see his face during the day. He was here, here, I told myself. So much of prayer is simply trying to stop, look, and listen.

But trying to see the face of God also means accepting whatever you find. As a diabetic, I need to test my blood-sugar levels on a regular basis. You can do it at home with a device called a glucometer. The higher your blood-sugar levels, the greater chance of complications down the road. Testing takes only a minute or so, and it's the best way to keep your levels under control, but I was afraid to test myself, afraid that I'd find out they were too high. (I know, dumb. More than dumb.) It was like a pop quiz I gave to myself. Had I been eating properly? Exercising enough? Days would go by, and then I'd finally grit my teeth, haul out the damn meter, prick my finger with a penlike lancing device and place a little bead of blood on the test strip. The glucometer would beep and begin processing the sugar level while a gray square blinked on the display panel. Ten seconds . . . twenty seconds . . . thirty seconds . . . Complications from diabetes include numbness, impotence, gangrene, blindness, and death. My heart would be pounding. Then at last the glucometer would give a little beep, and a number would jump out.

This also is the face of God, I told myself one morning, looking at the number. If I believed in God, if I really, really trusted him, then I had to trust in the reality he created for me. I shouldn't flinch from this testing. Religion isn't the opiate of the masses. In fact, it's just the opposite. It's stark realism, looking at yourself and God's creation without blinking or flinching or turning aside.

No Divisions, in other words, and that meant all the duties and errands in my life. I began to consider the local Walmart my spiritual proving ground. On Saturdays I would sometimes take the kids shopping. The store helped me test those ever-so-pleasant epiphanies I'd been enjoying just a few hours before.

The boys and I would usually go to Burger King for lunch. I'd still be tense from the work week, and it was usually crowded and noisy. One morning we got there right at noon, and the restaurant was filled with screaming kids and maybe thirty people in line. I hate waiting, but the boys loved Burger King's playscape, so I stood in line while they disappeared into the maze of plastic tunnels. I'd been up since four, and I was tired. I looked at the wait in front of me. What would Jesus do? How would he get through a Saturday with the kids, standing in line at Burger King?

Then I realized that Jesus had never been in a hurry, at least not the way we are. He lived in God time. What he accomplished in three years changed the world, but he never rushed, he never had a schedule, he never told his disciples to hurry up, even when he knew his mortal time was running out. He was always in action: moving, traveling, praying, taking care of others, and people were always interrupting him, breaking into his prayers, asking for healing even while he was on his way to heal someone else. But he never said, "I'll get back to you on that." He was never too busy.

So I stood in line, thinking about the patience and love of Christ, though I was still pissed.

Harrison wouldn't listen to reason. He was spending his time at school fooling around with the rowdiest kids instead of following directions and handing in his papers on time and completing his projects. In Colossians, I read, "Fathers, do not provoke your children so they may not become discouraged" (3:21). The more I talked, the more he slumped down in his chair with a dejected look. I looked at him and heard the tone of my voice, and I was worried for both of us.

I once saw a sign on a classroom wall at a Baptist Sunday school: "Prayer isn't heaven's delivery service, but rather a way for us to better love God." I began to think of prayer as an alignment, not a request, as a way to try to balance what I wanted with what I saw as God's will. Not that I usually could. But I noticed that when I stopped thinking about what Harrison *did* and focused on who he *was*, what I saw was a wonderfully decent, kind, and naturally intelligent young boy. He had a beautiful soul. It was all that simple. I was reassured.

Until the next day, that is. Then I started yelling again. I was angry with myself for being so angry, and I'll tell you something else: I was beginning to sound just like the Boss! Aaaah! As I lectured Harrison about homework, I heard the same irritation and cruel contempt creeping into my voice that I heard—or thought I heard—in the Boss's voice as she reviewed my work. Part of me wanted to humiliate my boy the same way I was humiliated at work. But that meant I was becoming the very person I couldn't stand! It was very depressing and very humbling to hear myself, though not humbling enough for me to actually stop.

One morning, trying to pray, I kept repeating the words, *Thy will be done*. An image came to me of Jesus brushing the hair from my face, kissing me very lightly on the forehead. *That's how I kiss Spencer and Harrison*, I thought, *or kiss Lauren to wake her up in the morning*. That's how my mother sometimes kissed me before I was older and I pushed her away. I realized for a moment that the more I could accept what God had given us in Harrison, the more I could give God's love back, reflected and re-reflected in our homes, our schools, in the mall on Saturday mornings.

My first Palm Sunday as a believer, I decided to walk the labyrinth downtown at the Methodist Center. I went upstairs to register. Nice people greeted me, took my name, and led me into a darkened auditorium. The labyrinth itself was marked out on a huge canvas sheet on the floor, fifty feet across. Quiet music. Small votive candles glowing in the corners. I took off my shoes and sat down for a bit. Centered. Relaxed. Then I entered the path marked on the canvas.

Several people were ahead of me, moving very slowly and deliberately around the canvas, their heads bowed. We were following a path through many twists and turns to the center of the labyrinth, then slowly retracing our steps back to the entrance. The whole process took thirty minutes, maybe an hour. I tried walking at basic meditation speed. Was I going too fast? This was a mediation, I reminded myself. I should stop yammering in my head, right? Did I lock my car? How long was I going to be here? I'd only been walking a few minutes, and now it looked as if I was almost at the center! Too fast! Slow down! Did I take a wrong turn? Okay, okay, relax. The path turned away. I was being steered back to the edge, almost where I began. Ulysses, catching sight of Ithaca before being blown off course again. So how much progress was I making? But no. There's no such thing as "progress." If I thought about progress, I wasn't making any.

But why was that woman tailgating me? I tried to speed up a bit. Oh hell, let her pass. She's on her path, I'm on mine. Right foot slowly, left foot slowly. I felt as if I were in the middle of the ocean. Right turn, left turn. Right brain, left brain. No sight of land, no sense of how far to go. Adrift. All my books and coffee. My intentions and ambitions. Was I finished? Had I barely begun? Would I ever get there?

And then, very quickly it seemed, the path was taking me toward the center. A few more turns and, bingo, there I was. Was this my destination? Had I "arrived?"

I paused. Then I slowly followed the path back out.

Afterwards I sat in the car for a moment before driving home. Where was I going now? I thought about something I'd once read by David Whyte: if you see your path clearly in front of you, it's not your path. It belongs to somebody else. You can find your own path only by walking it, and you find it only as you walk it. Maybe confusion is itself a path, at times. So follow the confusion. Be faithful to it.

A squirrel came jumping toward me across the lawn. Then froze, staring at nothing.

I felt dizzy but calm, like I'd spent a week in the country.

☙❧

Lauren and I were still avoiding any big discussions about God, but we couldn't stop sharing a bit what we were going through. How could we? One night she talked about growing up in Seattle, how she used to wander in the woods near her home, aching for something divine, though she didn't have a name or a shape for it. She told me she still had that ache, and I said I knew what she was talking about.

We were both trying so hard, and that was the problem, for me at least. Did I have faith? Sure, in my own will. Faith in my self-sufficiency. "I can do it by myself!" was my motto as a toddler. But now, after months of effort, I saw myself only as a sort of gray moth fluttering against a glass pane. And the more I pressed against the glass, the thicker it became, and it became thicker exactly where and to what degree I pressed. If I breathed on the glass, it clouded and thickened just slightly, just enough to stop me—moth wing pressed against moth wing. If I pushed harder, it turned into glass. And if I rammed my head against it (More books! More books! Think! Think, you idiot!!), it became a brick wall, hard against hard.

⚭

In *Iron and Silk* Mark Salzman talks about learning the martial arts, and he says, "Go to as many teachers as you can find." After Easter, I made an appointment to talk with Father Norm at the Episcopal church. We sat down in his office, and I rambled on for ten minutes, trying to explain what I'd been going through, telling him that I knew I was reading too fast, wanting to make progress and knowing that "progress" wasn't the point. He listened politely until I'd finished. Then he asked, puzzled, "Are you hard on yourself? I mean, as a rule? Why not just enjoy this conversion process?"

I beg your pardon! I'm going through a profound religious experience! I'm not just having fun! But Norm's point was reasonable. I was getting so focused that I was cross-eyed. With all my inner churning, was it God I was trying to take so seriously or just myself? A rabbinical saying goes: "In heaven, a person will have to account for every happiness he deliberately chose not to enjoy."

In fact, everything that Norm said was reasonable. Everyone at his church was reasonable. Every Episcopalian I'd ever met seemed reasonable. Norm explained to me that the Episcopal Church (or the Anglican Church as it was called in England) was based on three pillars: tradition, Scripture, and reason. Obviously, reason was a major part of its strength and goodness. I knew that most Protestant denominations had a radical heritage. Quakers used to literally quake. Shakers shook. Even Methodists were once firebrands, breaking away from the Anglicans and going off to minister to the coal miners in Wales. And the Lutherans, of course, were revolutionaries, igniting the Reformation. In time, however, like all radical movements, these denominations stabilized and became middle-class and reasonable. That was fine, I thought. The middle-class needs a church just as everyone else does. I was middle-class, and I appreciated that stability. It was what I valued most in my Methodist background. You'll never see a Methodist terrorist. When I go to a mainstream Protestant church, I know I'll usually be around people with their heads on straight, people who avoid extremes. Reason guides them. What could be more reasonable?

And that was the problem. Banging around inside my head and heart was a desire for an intensity that I just couldn't find at our neighborly Episcopal church. The Anglican/Episcopal culture offered moderation. I also knew that there were members of that church and Anglicans throughout the world with a faith far deeper, far more fervent than I might ever see, a faith that had supported their church for centuries. But still, I kept hankering for a church that was more intense, even if that intensity was completely unreasonable.

Type "Catholic and bizarre" into any search engine on the Internet and see what you get. I wanted a church that was cultivated and enlightened, a good place to raise the boys. But I was also drawn to the Catholic Church precisely because its culture included such an enormous spectrum of human behavior that was definitely not reasonable, even at times bizarre. I kept thinking about the Elia Kazan movie version of *A Streetcar Named Desire*. In one scene, Blanche Dubois is being confronted by Mitch. He's been interested in her, they've had a date, and Blanche has scattered hopes of marriage. But now Mitch has discovered that Blanche has what used to be called a checkered past.

"I thought you were straight!" he keeps complaining, repeating the word until finally she turns and says, "Straight? What's 'straight'? A line can be straight, or a street. But the heart of a human being?"

The Catholic Church and Catholic culture understand how unstraight the human heart can be. So do other churches, of course, but I felt that Catholic understanding was deeper, if only by the sheer weight of experience. Over the centuries, the Mother Church has seen too much—and been involved with too much, both good and bad—to be shocked with any little crooked thing I could offer. I felt that Episcopalian culture, in a very English-middle-class sort of way, avoided what was Definitely Not Nice. I was drawn—yes, I'll admit it; I was thrilled—by a culture that included weird customs and dark, intense mysteries. A church with nuns who spent every waking hour praying for the universe. A church that included the *Summa Theologica* but also hair shirts and cults of Mary and levitating saints and pilgrims crawling toward a shrine for miles on bloody knees, flagellating themselves until their backs were raw. (I'm being honest here, folks.) I grew up feeling out of place, but the Catholic Church, it seemed, had a place for everyone.

Yes, the Episcopal parishioners offered us a place in their church. But every so often, Lauren and I would be chatting along with them, and suddenly there was an uncomfortable silence. Oops. Once again we'd said something that seemed perfectly normal to us but was strange to them. I don't want to make us sound oh-so-unusual. We're basically a couple of suburban parents, middle-class to the bone. But I always felt we were like moose at that church, sort of loud and clumsy with big antlers, almost knocking over the coffee urn or the racks of literature. Everything we said seemed a bit too loud, too emphatic, too *too*. Sure, the Episcopalians were friendly now, but what if we *really* told them what was going on in our heads? Some members would understand. They might have the same thoughts themselves. But what about the others? What would they think of flagellation?

There were other reasons, maybe more important, why I couldn't join the Episcopal Church. One dark, rainy Sunday morning, I went to a Catholic church in west Austin. The priest was a large, serious-looking man with a Middle Eastern accent. During the Eucharistic prayer, as thunder rumbled quietly in the distance, he raised the Host, looked us all straight in the eye and said in a deep, steely voice, "This *is* my body. *Eat it!*" That was not a casual suggestion. That was a stone command to every Catholic in that room. I knew I was exactly where I belonged. Frankly, after years of self-centeredness, I probably needed to bend my neck to something greater than myself, both to God and to an institution, whether it all seemed reasonable or not.

In fact, I wanted a church and a theology that were completely and gloriously *unreasonable* in some respects, cutting across the logical grain and violating all normal borders of common sense. Like St. Augustine, I didn't want faith based on understanding, but understanding based on faith. Religious truth vaults over the plausible. That's why I fully accepted the Catholic dogma of transubstantiation, the belief that the Eucharistic Host and wine are really, truly, and literally changed into the body and blood of Christ during Mass. Of course it didn't "make sense." As a religious truth, why should it? I knew that some Catholics approached their faith through reason. Merton first accepted the existence of God after reading Étienne Gilson's book on scholastic philosophy. But I was attracted by what was paradoxical, to the mystery and not the logical argument. Father Norm was logical. He made sense. When we were talking about the Eucharist, he said nonchalantly, "Of course, it's only a symbol."

No, it's not! I thought, and at that moment, I decided I would never be an Episcopalian.

Smugness is the Great Catholic Sin, wrote Flannery O'Connor. Deep inside I nurtured the completely unfair— unreasonable?—notion that the Catholic Church with all its beliefs, including transubstantiation, was still the one true church. Call it smugness, call it spiritual snobbery, but I couldn't help seeing Episcopalians as JVCs, Junior Varsity Catholics. Father Norm told me that he felt he was a part of the apostolic succession of Christ. But I kept looking at his Roman collar, trying but never fully believing that he was actually a priest.

I didn't have the apostolic problem with Catholic priests or the Catholic Church. One day I attended a communion service at St. Edward's that was being celebrated by a deacon. The crowd was small, and Deacon Dick gathered everyone at the altar for the Eucharistic liturgy. He went through the liturgy, and everyone started sharing the body and blood of Christ. I stayed in the pews since as a non-Catholic I couldn't accept communion. I guess I looked kinda mournful out there by myself. Communion is supposed to be where we all share a blessing. So Dick walked over to me, made the sign of the cross on my forehead, blessed me in the name of the Father, the Son, and the Holy Spirit, and prayed that I would be filled with the love of God and the light of Christ.

Oh! I floated out of the chapel, almost trembling. *I've been blessed! And blessed by someone who's been blessed by a priest who'd been blessed by a priest who'd been blessed by a priest before that, blessings all the way back in an unbroken, two-thousand year-old chain to Jesus Christ, the Son of God.*

I'd never felt that way with any Protestant church or pastor. Yes, all churches, Protestant and Catholic, are part of the body of Christ, but at the same time, I couldn't, and still can't, shake the totally unreasonable feeling that only Catholicism is the real deal.

Ironically, even Lauren shared my feelings about the one, true church. "If you're going to join a church, go Catholic," she said. "It's the only game in town." But she also made it plain that at this point she wasn't interested in any Christian church at all. It was okay if I joined, okay that the boys went to church every Sunday, but leave her out of it.

I saw us both in our spiritual dune buggies racing across the desert plains, weaving across each other's tracks in a loose braid stretching back to the horizon. But how loose was this braid becoming? Sometimes it seemed as if we were veering closer and closer together, beginning to meet, and then we'd collide—"Bow down!" "Stand up!" "Humility!" "No! Freedom!"—and off we'd go again, veering off on our own paths. I began to realize that if this continued, someday, perhaps, we'd lose sight of each other altogether. How much latitude could we tolerate? How much disagreement could a marriage stand?

But then—oh, the mysteries of marriage—it was Lauren who kept encouraging me to join the church and find a parish where I could begin the process of initiation. She mentioned our friend Kelly several times. Kelly was a cradle Catholic who was guiding her oldest daughter through first communion, and they attended St. Austin's near the university. She wanted to refresh her knowledge of her faith, so she was taking a series of classes during the summer called the Faith of Catholics. She had mentioned to Lauren that she always felt so calm and happy after the classes. The instructor was great.

"Why don't you go to St. Austin's?" Lauren suggested. I told her I'd been there before. I didn't like the architecture. The church was built in a plain, unadorned style out of the early fifties, very beige and colorless it seemed to me, though at the time it was probably the latest word in "modern" design.

I also didn't like the way St. Austin's conducted their Mass. I was still in my Hollywood period at the time: the little Masses at St. Ed's were sweet, but Sunday required a high Mass like the ones you saw in the movies. At St. Austin's, the Mass was only so-so high. They had announcements at the end of services, all very casual it seemed to me. The day I was there, they even sang happy birthday to the choir leader. I'd stick with a Real Catholic Parish that took itself seriously.

St. Ed's didn't have a full program for joining the church, but when I asked Deacon Dick about other parishes, he asked, "Why don't you go to St. Austin's?" He told me I'd probably fit well. It was a diverse community that included teachers, scholars, and university students. "The parish is run by the Paulist fathers," he added. "I think you'd like them. They're a pretty down-to-earth bunch of guys."

Fair enough. I'd go to St. Austin's, check out the classes, see if I felt it was the right choice. I told Lauren, "They might have a good program for entering the church." Then I added with a knock-on-wood feeling, "That's assuming I decide to become Catholic."

"You already are," she said. "Don't know what kind, though. We'll see."

7

Faith of Catholics

On a Sunday morning in June, I went back to St. Austin's. I still didn't like the architecture, but a lot of parish members at St. Austin's probably thought it was perfectly lovely. There were nice touches: icons of St. Augustine of Canterbury and Our Lady of Perpetual Help. A Lady chapel was to the left of the altar. I could live with this. I'd focus on the liturgy and not the decor.

I sat down in one of the back pews. After a few moments I felt a tap on the shoulder. I turned around, and there was our friend Kelly! She had both daughters with her. Running into Kelly seemed like a good sign. After Mass we went over to the reception hall next door and sat down with doughnuts and coffee.

I'd been around Catholic Masses for six months by now, but I had never been around Catholics socially. Certainly not when I was growing up, and not even now. Like my early days in recovery, I'd just been showing up for Mass, then leaving immediately. But here I was, sitting down with a whole tribe of them. Everywhere I looked, I saw Catholics: Catholic men, Catholic women, little Catholic kids eating Catholic doughnuts. I sipped my Catholic coffee. Funny, but it tasted normal, like your basic nonprofit coffee. I put some Catholic nondairy creamer in my cup. Did Catholics put more, maybe less, sugar in their coffee? The crowd looked normal, but I felt like an anthropologist. I glanced casually around the room, hoping to catch some sign or mannerism, a Catholic secret handshake that would betray them.

I'd always wondered what Catholics had in their homes. Maybe candles everywhere. Crucifixes hanging over their beds. Bloody paintings over the mantelpiece. My mind wandered. What was Catholic sex like? Furtive but deliciously intense? Wasn't guilt the best aphrodisiac? I had watched Catholic women during the service, batting away wildly inappropriate speculations, until the thought occurred, *Hey, dummy, I'm married to a Catholic. We have two kids.*

Nothing bizarre happened as Kelly and I talked, though I still felt I was in the middle of something vaguely outlandish, even taboo. She told me about the parish's Faith of Catholics classes that she was attending. "I always feel so *good* afterward, and I think you'd like Michael. He's the instructor."

I made an appointment with Michael the next week. As I walked down the hallway toward his office, I thought of all the other meetings and sessions I'd gone to in the past: conferences with college professors, business meetings, appointments with psychiatrists, the thousands of recovery meetings I'd attended, the years of t'ai chi lessons in New York lofts. And here I was, beginning again. Maybe this could be my last major beginning, the true one I'd been trying to find all along.

Michael greeted me at the doorway, and we sat down. He was a man my own age, with a dapper goatee and a smiling face. Later I learned that his confirmation name was Peter and that he was, indeed, a kind of gatekeeper. He seemed friendly and open, though I noticed his eyes were very clear and assessing. "Now then," he said, "what brings you to St. Austin's?"

"Basically I'm here because I've fallen in love," I said. I told him about the monastery, about coming back, and about my need to go to Mass. I talked about all the feelings kicked up by going to Mass, how I'd become focused—obsessed?—with the Host, how communion seemed more important than anything else right now. It all came flooding out with me getting all worked up as I talked. All the while, he was smiling, nodding, as if he knew exactly what I meant.

We talked for an hour, and then we continued to meet over the summer. He always seemed to have time for another appointment. I was also going to his Wednesday-night classes, which covered the history of the church, basic doctrine, Scripture, Catholic culture, all your basic introductory stuff. My sessions with Michael, along with the classes and Sunday Mass, became the high points of my week.

We talked about big things and little things, Catholic trivia and the Really Big Questions. We talked about purgatory. (Salvation to Catholics isn't necessarily a binary, go/no-go condition at death. Sometimes we need a bit more time to sort things out and make amends.) We talked about limbo. (No, it's not a taught doctrine of the church. Never was.) We talked about why priests are celibate (short answer: a legacy from the early monastic tradition of the church and an expression of commitment to a life of service) and why Catholics cross themselves with holy water entering and leaving church (to remind us of the cleansing waters of baptism on our way in and our mission to love and serve the Lord on our way out).

I talked about my compulsion to control the process I was entering, and I told him about my creeping pride in how much I'd read and learned since last November. If you're a bookish person, I asked, how do you escape being arrogant about your learning? He offered that the Jesuits deal with the same issues. They know their Aquinas backward and forward, but they understand that helping the poor and

homeless can teach them aspects of faith more clearly than any seminary theologian.

We talked about more things than I can remember, more than my
notes covered. But along with all the facts about history, doctrine,
and culture, I began to learn through Michael what it means to be
a Catholic person, a living member of the church. He offered me a
model of a well-informed faith, but there was more. When I think of
the single most valuable thing he gave me, I think it was his smile.
It was fresh and lopsided, kind of goofy, the way it is with people
who don't take themselves too seriously. It was the welcoming spirit
of someone who's found something absolutely wonderful and wants
to share it. Here was a man with good news, I thought, news still
fresh after two thousand years. He was the kid on the playground who
rushes up to you, almost ready to bust, saying, "Hey! Guess what?"
And I was the kid he was talking to, hanging on his words.

I had issues with some church doctrines such as birth control, gay
sexuality, women as priests—the usual sticking points of many, though
not all, North American Catholics these days. But I learned that the
church calls us to honor these issues by sincerely examining, understanding, and even wrestling with what it teaches. You don't simply agree or disagree. You read church doctrine and Scripture. You
pray. You fully articulate your own position and think through issues
you might have with the church. Instead of settling for cafeteria-style
Catholicism, you hold an ongoing dialogue that preserves and even
enriches your relationship with the church. From the outside, the
church might look like a solid, monolithic pyramid with big pope on
top and all these itsy-bitsy Catholics running around the bottom like
ants. But I was learning that from the inside, it was much more like a
family. Yes, you defer to the head of the family, but this doesn't mean
you check your brain, or your heart, at the door. Besides, when all was

said and done, I had no problem accepting the authority of Rome. Why join a church where you can be a member simply by showing up?

The Catholic faith I saw was fantastically rich, one of Michael's favorite words. Catholicism was giving me answers that were deeply satisfying without being reductionistic. One day, Michael said, just in passing, that the purpose of life was "to become the person God wants you to be." At that moment, a question I'd been asking all my life was quietly and fully answered. I had many moments like that in the months that followed the initial meeting with Michael. I still do.

Not all the answers are simple or comforting. Michael told me, "God is a gentle lover. He doesn't use force; that wouldn't be love. He approaches us persistently but quietly. And he loves us completely without condition." That sounded great to me. That was the honeymoon part. But Michael also told me, "You have to become fully open to this love. God wants every speck, every last drop of you, and he's not satisfied with half measures." That was the challenge: no divisions, no holding back. I could find the full measure of God's love only in how I applied it to my life. Jesus was always asking people what they were going to *do* with God's love. The parables never ended with "They lived happily ever after." Rather, the parables emphasized action, movement, and choices, very hard choices sometimes, with even harder consequences.

We talked about hell. Yes, the Catholic Church teaches that there is a hell. Hell isn't a very fashionable idea these days. But it's linked to the broader idea that God doesn't treat us like children. We grow up to be conscious adults, and we have to make choices. Not believing in hell would be to deny free will. Hell also is a way to describe what it means to be completely turned away from God. However, Michael pointed out that in all her history, the church has named hundreds that are believed to be in heaven—but she hasn't asserted that any human is in hell.

We talked about excommunication, which still happens, occasionally. You get a letter from your bishop. You're formally and irrevocably barred from ever taking communion again or participating in the church in any way. But it happens these days only in extreme cases, where, let's say, someone takes a very public and persistent stance against the church.

Toward the end of the summer, we talked more about who could join the church. Could a thoroughly evil person, a Hitler (himself from a Catholic family) be admitted? Yes, Michael said, adding if—he emphasized this—if that person clearly and fully put a distance between himself and his past. Could a Pol Pot, his hands dripping with blood? Yes. Could a couple who'd had an abortion? Yes, he said. All the sacraments, particularly those of initiation, were about new life. It could be painful to begin that new life, to take responsibility for what you'd done in the past, but the offer and possibility of rebirth were always extended through the sacrament and celebrated through it.

The invitation to join the church wouldn't be casual. Becoming Catholic isn't like joining a bowling league. It is, in every sense of the phrase, *for life*. I had the feeling that I was returning to an ocean I had always known about but never touched, and here I was on the beach and everything else—the sand, the salt smell in the air, the waves—was talking to me at a primal level and whispering *yes* and telling me, clearly and undeniably, "Welcome home."

⌒✖⌒

I never had any hesitation about wanting to join the church, but let me make one thing clear: my conversion was never a defined process. It was never like a decision tree on the telephone—"For spiritual truth, press one . . . For Christianity, press two . . . For entering the Catholic Church, press three, and someone will assist you . . ." Some days, a lot of days, it seemed that nothing was happening according to plan, my plan anyway.

Lauren and I were still going through our theological do-si-do, me moving toward the church as she moved away. Or maybe it was more like a revolving door: the more I pushed in on my side, the more she was propelled out on her side, and vice versa. It wasn't easy for me to watch this, and it wasn't easy for her. She had the freedom to follow her own path, but she also probably felt that she was always outgunned in a way. Here was her husband not only going through a major conversion but assuming the mantle of the very church she grew up in. She might not be a follower, but she had a lifetime of family feelings about the church. She was still Catholic at the cellular level. I was seeking to be one with a billion other Catholics around the world. Where was her group, now that she was moving away from the church?

Lauren had gone to the first Faith of Catholic class with me and talked about what she felt were the Bad Old Days of the church, all those mean nuns and arrogant priests and the parishioners who attended Mass on automatic pilot. Michael smiled and conceded that yes, the church had needed to change. "What about the role of women in the church?" Lauren asked. Yes, he added, it was still changing and always would. After class, Lauren thanked him and told me she thought he was a wonderful teacher, but she didn't attend any more classes.

I knew that her spiritual commitment to finding her own path was as deep as mine, if not deeper. I also knew that I wasn't going to convert her. How was I going to be Defender of the Faith, me with my two bits' worth of knowledge, faith, and experience? But I wanted her to know that the church I'd discovered was a new church, not the one she had known as a child. I had read that even if somebody grew up in a faith community, they had to go through a second conversion, often in their twenties or thirties. They had to basically "rejoin" the church, rethinking their faith and readjusting to a new role as an adult member of their church. Lauren had never gone through this second conversion. I wanted to think that she represented a classic case of a child's faith that had never made the transition, the "second conversion" to the faith of an adult.

On Sunday, while the boys were watching TV in the front room, Lauren and I found ourselves with a few precious moments when we could talk. We went to the back bedroom and sat next to the bay window, next to her bookshelves.

"You really think that if you're patient enough, I'll get this New Age thinking out of my system and return to the church, don't you?" she asked.

"The thought crossed my mind."

"Sweetie, I love you and support you. I think that the church, *for you*, mind you, is wonderful. But—and I don't want this to sound condescending—I went through what you're going through when I was eight or nine. I was truly, madly, deeply in love with the church, with all its beauty and glory and majesty. Jesus was my best friend." She pointed to her Sacred Heart painting that I'd put over her side of the bed. "I'd talk to him for hours when I was a teenager. That painting was just like a telephone."

"So what happened?"

"Life happened. You know all that. I got married, divorced. Drugs. Alcohol. But my point is that I've already gone through everything you're going through, and now I need something more, something . . . else."

I felt the same way about her New Age reading. Been there. Odd how we were becoming reverse images of each other. But maybe we could come to common terms, somehow.

"Wait a minute," I said, going to my study and coming back with a copy of the church's *Declaration on the Relationship of the Church to*

Non-Christian Religions. I found one paragraph in particular that I had underlined:

> The Catholic Church rejects nothing which is true and holy in these religions. It looks with sincere respect upon those ways of conduct and of life, those rules and teachings which, though differing in many particulars from what it holds and sets forth, nevertheless . . .

I was losing her. "Wait. Here's the good part," I said.

> . . . nevertheless often reflect a ray of that Truth which enlightens all people.

"A *ray*?" she said. "That's condescending. Here, let me see that." She took the book from me and read the next sentence.

> Indeed, it proclaims and ever must proclaim Christ, "the way, the truth, and the life," in whom everyone finds the fullness of religious life, and in whom God has reconciled all things.

She handed the book back. "So truth to the church is always with a capital 'T' and that stands for Christ."

"So? The Church can't accept just everything, willy-nilly. You don't want just the lowest common denominator. You have to make choices." Then I played my favorite trump card. "It's like love. Love is biased. I love you, and I think you're the most interesting woman I know. I'm not disparaging other women. It's just that you're the one I love. So I acknowledge that other faiths can be valid, but I'm still focused on my own, simply because it's the one I love."

"And I respect that. But all I'm asking is that you respect where I'm going as well."

"Where's that?"

"I don't know. But it ain't Catholic."

"Okay, maybe we can look at it this way. From what I can see, most religions, certainly Catholicism, are either vertical or horizontal or some mixture. Usually a mixture. The Catholic Church you knew as a child was way vertical. It was very hierarchical and emphasized a God that was up there, transcendent and powerful. Big God, little me. Taken to the extreme, you just had guilt and this mechanical obedience, and you had a strong emphasis on submission."

"You're telling me."

"But!" I said brightly, "now you have a church that's more balanced between the vertical and the horizontal. We still celebrate a transcendent God, but we also celebrate the immanence of God. He's up there, but he's down here, too, all around us. We're the image of God as well as God's children. You're simply going all the way toward a horizontal, immanent view."

"It's not simple, thank you very much, and I'm going a lot further than that. I know this is a cliché these days, but I truly feel I can be spiritual without being religious."

"But what's being 'spiritual'? Look at this New Age stuff," I said, pointing to the bookshelf. "Look at these titles. You haven't bought a book for the last two years that didn't have 'you,' or 'your' in the title. It's a me-me-me theology." I was getting up a head of steam. "I'm sorry but it seems like the worst of modern, self-centered, self-indulgent American culture. Look here!" I pointed to one book, *Miracles on Demand*. "Look at that! The title says it all! All this stuff is about empowerment and control. That's nothing but pure ego. You wind up just being by yourself!"

I could see her starting to say something; then she paused and said, "I never see myself as alone. God, or Goddess, or the Great Mother, whatever word you want to use, the Divine is always with me."

I tried to back off a bit. "Well, you were talking about being spiritual, but frankly, the most spiritual people I know these days *are* religious!" That sounded harder than I intended.

"I'll be frank, too. I can't go back to a church with such a bloody history. Look at the—"

"I know. The inquisitions, the crusades. Yes, yes. But the church reflects the society it serves, for better or worse. It tries to do its best, but as somebody, a monk I think, said, 'Of course the church is a sinful institution. How could it not be?'"

"Somehow that just sounds too easy," she said. "Let me show you something." She went to the bookshelf and found a passage from *A Woman's Journey to God* by Joan Borysenko:

> On the plane to India, I had read about the Portuguese Inquisition in Goa on India's west coast. The inquisitors forced perfectly happy, God-centered Hindus to renounce their religion and become Christian. If the converted "Christians" were caught worshipping their own gods, they were tortured and killed. One image in particular was seared onto my brain. The inquisitors cut off the eyelids of parents so that they could not shut out the sight of their children being slowly dismembered in front of them. The Inquisition in India lasted into the late 1800s.

"The *late 1800s*," she said again, putting the book down.

"Okay," I said. "What can I say to that? But the church isn't a part of things like that anymore. It's changed, and it keeps on changing."

"Not enough. And not fast enough. Besides, it's a very structured organization. It's like a corporation."

"Fine. That's why I don't mind working for a corporation. Everybody defers to someone else. Staff reports to management, management reports to the CEO, and even the CEO is responsible to the board and the stockholders. In the church, everyone defers to the pope, and the pope reports to God."

"How long would I last in a corporation?"

"About a day. You'd pick a fight with somebody. You wouldn't fit in."

"Exactly."

"But can you see what I'm saying? Deferring to an authority isn't abuse. It's, well, deference."

"But I still don't want to go to a Mass where the priest is up there running the show."

"But he's up there serving all of us as a servant of Christ."

"He's still up there, and we're down in the pews, taking orders. No, I still see the church as a confinement. It's a box. A glorious one, a lovely one, but a box."

"I don't see it that way."

"But don't you feel that it takes away your freedom?" She seemed genuinely perplexed.

"Well, I've been thinking about this. To me, the church is more like a trellis. I'm like that wisteria we have in the backyard. For years I was growing, sending out these feelers, all these branches, but I was just sprawling around. It was only when I found the framework of the church that I had something to support my growth. The church directs where I can grow, but it allows me to grow much higher and send my roots down deeper than I would have otherwise. It allows me to be closer to everything I've been straining toward all along, up to the light and down to the earth. It doesn't force me to be someone else. In fact, I'm more myself than I've ever been."

"That's wonderful—for you," she said. "But the church is still a hierarchy, and that's the point, finally." She leaned forward, like Carmen at the monastery. "The church is a male-dominated hierarchy. It's more than whether women are allowed to be priests. It's the whole fact that it's run by men. It's a guy thing, and I think it always will be, at least in our lifetimes. It will always have this hierarchical male structure."

"Are we talking about religion now or sexual politics?"

"Sexual politics should be an outgrowth of your spirituality, right?"

"Agreed. But what about all those generations of strong women in the church?" I asked.

"The great women saints? All those tough nuns?"

"God bless 'em, truly. But I can't be a part of that and keep my own faith alive."

I couldn't convince Lauren, but I kept thinking about what she had said about the sins of the church. Even Cardinal Joseph Ratzinger, before he became Pope Benedict XVI, had said as much:

> The centuries of the Church's history are so filled with human failure that we can quite understand Dante's ghastly vision of the Babylonian whore sitting in the Church's chariot; and the dreadful words of William of Auvergne, Bishop of Paris in the thirteenth century, seem perfectly comprehensible. William said that the barbarism of the Church must make everyone who saw it go rigid with horror: "Bride she is no more, but a monster of frightful ugliness and horror. . . ."

I thought about that and Borysenko's quote. And all the violence carried out in the name of the church. And the misery it's overlooked or even inflicted. I thought about uncaring priests, sadistic priests, priests sexually abusing children and adults. I thought about how many times the church has apparently lost sight of the most obvious commandments of Christ. As Ratzinger put it, "for many people today, the Church has become the main obstacle to belief."

But Ratzinger also pointed out that the holiness of the church doesn't mean that it's "spotless" but rather that it offers a grace that God continues to give us, despite the imperfections of its members. Christ himself mingled with sinners, and God has always refused to keep his distance from us. Instead, through Jesus, he plunged into the center of what was darkest in our hearts and institutions. He endured our deliberate violence against everything divine. And all the while, he taught forgiveness. Not limp tolerance, mind you. He roared. He overturned tables. He preached revolution. But he also reminded us that bitter, unforgiving criticism is driven not by righteousness but by mere pride. He showed us that more often than not, humility demands reform rather than flat out rejection.

Of course, if I really wanted to get humble, I'd have to keep reminding myself how convenient it would be for me to join the church, and to join it at this point in my life. It was convenient that I was a male because the church was run, at least formally, by men. It was convenient that most of these men were white, straight men of European descent, just like me. It was also convenient that Lauren and I were married and past our childbearing years, and that we had already made clinically certain we weren't going to have any more kids. The whole premarital sex/contraception/abortion argument was no longer an issue that could affect us directly.

It was also convenient that our family wasn't facing any major problems or tragedies. We were all more or less healthy, I had a job, and we had a nice home. When I started my conversion, I had called up my friend Jack from grad school. He was happy to hear that I wanted to join the church. "I'm surprised it took you this long," he said. But at one point, I was rattling along about the glory of God and his plans for us and I suggested that maybe he could also find a faith community. His wife had been diagnosed with a fatal disorder. Most patients with her condition have only a few years to live. I was thinking that a church might be a help to both of them. He thanked me but declined. He had no inclination to find Jesus quite yet. I pressed on, saying that every path was just a step at a time. He replied patiently, "You know, if you had to deal with a diagnosis like hers, you might not be joining the church right now."

So, yes, joining the church was convenient for me at all levels, in all ways. But I hoped I was joining out of more than convenience. Like when I fell in love with Lauren, everything about the church was a natural fit. The sacraments were the perfect union of the visible and invisible, something I'd been trying to find all my life. It was a mediational church, with a priesthood serving as mediators. As with a corporation, I could see where I stood, somewhere between self-control and deference, and I had no problem deferring to the priests. Why should I? They were pros. They had pledged their lives to the church, and I respected that. Finally, the Catholic Church was communal, and that, too, seemed the best path I could take. I needed family, and the communal culture ("You're not a Catholic by yourself.") would keep me from staying too long in my study.

Those were the official reasons I gave when people asked me about the church. But I had one last reason, maybe more important than all the rest: I wanted to become a Catholic simply because I thought I could. I hadn't been struck with any blinding insights on my road to Damascus. Rather, my Catholic path was—and still is—guided by a gradual light, a revelation by slow degrees that continues to open me up. Becoming Catholic didn't necessarily require a leap of faith. I could crawl, Mass to Mass and practice to practice. The Mother Church seems to understand the value of "going through the motions," celebrating the physical practice as much as the inner conviction of being Christian. That struck me as one of the main glories of the liturgies. The very motions that some critics say are dry and mechanical were, for me, first steps that I could handle. The church, both in structure and culture, accommodated my limits and confusions while still encouraging me to move just a little bit further and deeper into faith. Regardless of what happened on any given day, I could always go to Mass, kneel and pray, cross myself, and know that I was participating in the church in a way that it recognized as significant and even crucial.

I said all this to Michael when I met with him at the end of the summer. Yes, I wanted to join, though I couldn't say I had crossed any major thresholds. All I could claim was my big toe over the threshold of the church. "Fine," he said, smiling, looking slightly inscrutable. He didn't seem bothered by anything I said. He didn't even seem surprised; perhaps my process was pretty obvious.

I told him that I didn't know what to expect of God. But I also told him that I knew that God had wonderful things in store for me and that I should wear this statement of faith like a shirt and be identified with it.

Still, I kept thinking about whether I was an appropriate candidate for the church, and I was grateful that I'd even been invited to start the process. Maybe I could sneak in under their radar. Maybe I'd luck out. Maybe they wouldn't ask me too many questions. Of course, the important questions would be asked only by God.

8

Rites of Welcome

The initiation process, called the Rite of Christian Initiation of Adults, or RCIA, had its kick-off meeting in October with a retreat on a Sunday morning. The retreat would be followed by a Rite of Acceptance and Welcome at 11:30 Mass. I'd never been on an organized retreat like this before. Would we go off to the woods? I wanted someplace physically remote. I thought of hermit huts and pilgrimages, people in habits trudging along dirt roads. Walking staffs. Begging bowls. That sort of thing.

We gathered in the meeting hall at 9:00. Then we made our pilgrimage by walking across the alley to the St. Austin school gym. Not very woodsy, but it was quiet and certainly big enough.

At the gym, Michael went over the five main stages of the RCIA:

- Period of Evangelization and Precatechumenate, during which people ask questions and receive basic instruction.

- Period of the Catechumenate that begins with the Rite of Acceptance and Welcome and provides further instruction about Christianity and the church. It's also a period in which initiates can learn more about what it means to live as a Catholic.

- Period of Purification and Enlightenment that includes the Rite of Election whereby the church formally ratifies the readiness of the initiates to proceed.

- Sacraments of Initiation at Easter, when the initiates are accepted into the church.

- There would also be a kind of warm-down period after Easter called *Mystagogia*, during which the new members can receive additional instruction and hand-holding that help ease their way into their new lives as Catholics.

With our schedules in hand, we broke into small groups scattered across the gym floor and talked about why we were thinking about joining the church. I told my story and listened to others. One man had been a member of the parish with his wife for thirteen years but was Lutheran. Then one night he had a dream. He didn't tell us what was in the dream, but here he was, ready finally to join. Another man was Islamic, and he said that Christianity was calling him more strongly now than Islam. Several members of the circle were newly married or engaged couples, with the cradle Catholic acting as sponsor to the initiate.

My own assigned sponsor didn't show up, so they grabbed Kevin from the RCIA team of helpers. Kevin would serve as my proxy sponsor for the day. This Rite would be a dramatic first step. We would have to get up in front of the entire congregation—gulp—and tell what we wanted from God and from the parish community. Then we'd be blessed.

At 11:30, we made our pilgrimage back across the alley and into the church. In the middle of Mass, we got up and faced a crowd of about five hundred people. Actually, the church looked small from the altar steps. What do we ask of God? What do we ask of this congregation?

"Please hold my hand," I said. "I need your help in leading me along this process." I added, "This is scary," and it was.

After everyone had a turn at the mike, initiates and sponsors faced one another for the signing of the cross. We were looking into one another's eyes. In this society, we rarely ever look, I mean really *look* into another person's eyes for any extended time, even as lovers. I remember once going through an introductory meeting for Scientology. We began with a Be-Here-Now exercise in which you sat in a chair across from someone else and simply stared at him, eyeball to eyeball, for five minutes or so. That was thirty years ago, but I still remember the fellow I sat with: his face, his expression, even the color of his eyes.

Now I was staring into Kevin's eyes. Lots of energy there. He was a West Point graduate, former soldier. Walking across the alley, he had patted me firmly on the back and told me, clearly, definitely, that yes, I was a blessing to the church. He radiated a bracing, military optimism that said, "Soldier, you can do this!"

At the Rite during Mass, we all stood on the altar steps, and Father P.J. carried us through the process which culminated in the signing of the cross:

> Receive the cross on your forehead.
> It is Christ himself who now strengthens you
> with this sign of his love.
> Learn to know and follow him.

Kevin made the sign of the cross over my forehead. Then—and this was the great part—P.J. kept going:

> Receive the sign of the cross on your ears
> that you may hear the voice of the Lord. . . .
>
> Receive the sign of the cross on your eyes . . .
> that you may see the glory of God.

> Receive the sign of the cross on your lips
> that you may respond to the word of God. . . .

Kevin was signing me over and over, on my ears, my eyes (I took off my glasses. I wanted the actual feel of his fingers on my eyelids), on my lips and then my heart, on both shoulders, both hands, and finally both of my feet. At the end of the rite, I felt as if I were in a full suit of armor. I glittered slightly as I walked, and I had the clear sense that, whatever happened, I wouldn't be going through this alone.

As the weeks went by, I could see that the RCIA was a carefully, even lovingly designed rite of passage. All through the process we were blessed and prayed over and blessed and welcomed and blessed even more. At the beginning of Lent we would even be exorcised. Every Sunday we were blessed and "sung out of the church" as we left for our discussion, walking down the aisles with the congregation on both sides singing:

> Go now in peace, go now in peace.
> Christ will be your way, your truth, your life.

I started feeling almost like a rock star. People from the parish, people I didn't even know, would come up to me and pat me on the back. It was great. Toward Easter, I even got cards and letters wishing me well.

At the same time, we were always aware that we were still on the outside, waiting for final acceptance in the church. For me, this was clearest at Mass when we had to leave just before supper. Everyone else would stay and receive communion; we had homework instead. I appreciated that fact, and I could see the wisdom in limiting communion to Catholics. Some would disagree. Alicia, my Episcopalian friend, had a major beef with limited Catholic communion. She told me about weddings, even funerals, that had been divided between Catholics and Protestants where one side of the family was kept from receiving communion. I justified the position by saying that it was a symbol of union, and until the Catholic and Protestant sides of Christianity were truly reunited, it wouldn't make symbolic sense for us to share the Eucharist. Besides, many Protestants didn't consider the Host to be the true body of Christ the way Catholics did (when did I start sounding like a theologian?) so they wouldn't be receiving the Host in the same spirit or understanding. She didn't buy it.

I could have added that having to wait to receive communion was a very effective part of my initiation. The church is a wise psychologist, and over time, she's learned what works and what doesn't. By having to wait, I was, as it were, saving myself for marriage. When Easter finally came and I took the body of Christ into my own body for the very first time, the experience would be all the more powerful from having waited for almost a year and a half.

⌒⧜⌒

My designated sponsor never showed up, so Michael asked Ted, one of the RCIA volunteers, to fill in. Ted was about my age, a large man with a full beard and a reassuring manner—a grandfather. As we went through the RCIA together, I thought of the method that Indians have developed to tame young, wild elephants to work in the logging camps. After being captured, the younger elephant is matched with an older one who's been working for years. The two are lashed together side by side and go through their work that way, day after day, until the younger one calms down and learns the drill. Ted was a cradle Catholic and had volunteered in the church for many years. I took advantage of his calm presence and gravity as I bounced through the next nine months, and he reminded me that quiet dependability was always more important than mere enthusiasm.

Ted and other men in the parish were my role models for being a Catholic man. At age forty-nine, I felt like a gawky adolescent as I prepared to enter the church. Catholics belonged to a very old and complex tribe. I needed to learn how to drink my Catholic coffee as much as to understand the theology, the prayers, or anything else. It was reassuring to be surrounded by men like Ted as well as Michael, Kevin, and others. These were solid, stand-up guys who also seemed to have a leg up on keeping that "strong but sensitive" balance that American guys are edging toward, inch by inch. "Catholic men": I liked the sound of that phrase.

I also learned a lot about being Catholic simply by hanging around the courtyard between Masses on Sunday. The church is next to a garden courtyard, with administration buildings on the other side. The area is pleasant and secluded from the street, with large beds of well-tended roses and a fountain in the middle.

Talking in the courtyard to the parishioners or just looking at the crowd from the edges, I saw qualities that seemed to me distinctly Catholic. In some Protestant churches, there's an unrelenting cheerfulness that drives me up the wall. As individuals, Protestants were of course as complex as anyone else, and as a convert, I might have been exaggerating differences between my past and present life. But in terms of church culture, I thought that Protestants feel more obligated to put on a happy face every Sunday. If you were a believer, then you showed it, in all good conscience, by being upbeat all the way.

Perhaps because Catholic culture was older, it seemed (to me at least, with all the enthusiasm and bias of a recent convert) to acknowledge and accommodate a greater range of feelings. The general tone at St. Austin's was always friendly and lively, of course. This was church, after all. People hugged and laughed. Children played around the fountain, eating their Catholic doughnuts. But sometimes I'd catch a glimpse of some of the older members at the edge of the crowd, maybe when they didn't know anyone was looking. Their faces would settle for a moment into what looked like sternness or disappointment or even a much darker expression, like a doctor recognizing cancer in an X-ray. I saw that especially in the older nuns and priests. Then somebody would walk up, say hi, and instantly their faces would brighten, as cheerful as ever, and the cheerfulness seemed genuine. One of the RCIA instructors once told us that when we approach God's light, his light becomes more apparent in our soul, but it also means that the shadows inside us become more clearly defined. That's what some of these older parish members seemed like—high-contrast photographs with strong light and strong shadows.

So hanging out with the parish was an important part of my catechesis. I'd be chatting along, saying something I thought was terribly significant, and then I would get this bemused look or an ever so slightly raised eyebrow. Instantly, three months of reading and thinking would be invalidated. Oops. Wrong way. Detour, back up. The point of my learning was not just amassing Catholic factoids but discovering how to live as a Catholic Christian. I could learn by reading and listening, but I could learn more by being around other Catholics and watching their faces, especially those eyebrows.

At the center of this parish family are our priests: Fathers Alan, Tom, and P.J. Alan is the youngest, and he's especially popular with the college students and twentysomething parish members. He had turned away from a promising career in advertising to become a priest. He once told Lauren and me that he had thrown away his business Rolodex when he entered the seminary. "It even contained Tom

Cruise's home phone number," he said. The man is well over six feet tall and completely bald. I always think of a lighthouse. He is an excellent communicator, more concerned with getting his message across than with priestly decorum. He can grace a homily with the theme song from *The Brady Bunch*. He also does a pretty decent Elvis imitation, singing to the congregation about a hunka-hunka-burnin' love as P.J. tries not to roll his eyes. But as Alan entertains us, doing his holy goof for God, I can see that underneath he's as serious as a surgeon. He might be laughing at himself, but he's not laughing at anything about faith, the church, or his role as a priest.

Tom is a bearlike man with a deep, bass voice. He's been a priest for more than twenty-five years. His grandfather was an Irish cop in New York, and he's one of the chaplains at the Austin Police Department. As I watched him work with the parish, I felt that he'd seen a lot of sadness along the way in many people, including himself perhaps. I knew more than a few parishioners who chose him as their confessor. His homilies are delivered in slow, measured tones, never rushed, and months later, I still remember his phrases and how he said them.

P.J. is the pastor, the boss of the parish. He's a planner and visionary, responsible for everything that goes on in the parish community. A former navy chaplain, a military guy, he can be a stickler for detail. That's his job, after all. When he presides at Mass, it seems that he's trying to pay attention to every movement and gesture, not because it's the drill but because he wants to celebrate the ritual every time as if for the first time.

All three priests are Paulist fathers, something I appreciated more as I learned more about their order. They serve at a parish in the diocese of Austin at the request of our local bishop, but they report directly to the head of the Paulist order. I've always felt comfortable with the Paulists. The order was founded by Isaac Hecker, a convert from a Methodist family, like me. His father was even a grain dealer, just like my grandfather. What's more, Paulists have always been focused on communication—writing, publishing, video, websites—just as I have in business. So thinking about me and St. Austin's and the Paulists, it all seemed meant to be.

c∞ϱ

As I went through the RCIA classes, I felt as if I were in school again. Old instincts poked their noses up. I knew that finding God is not a competitive sport. But I still wanted to be an achiever, one of the brightest lights in the class. I wanted to impress the priests. I wanted to impress Michael. I wanted to be like Christ among the elders or the Pharisees, astonishing everyone with my twenty-five cents' worth of wisdom and deep understanding.

But from the beginning I knew this course was going to be different. God does judge us, but there would be no grades given out at Easter. I couldn't read or talk my way to heaven. So did I act as if I could? Well, of course. I prepped for every Sunday discussion and started rehearsing my casual, off-the-cuff remarks several days in advance. Some of this was well intentioned; I felt a sort of professorial obligation to help the class along. I was one of the oldest members of the class. I'd also had any shyness about talking in front of a group drummed out of me by years of meetings in recovery. If you can deliver a drunkalogue about your incredibly stupid drinking past, you can usually get up in front of anybody and talk about anything. The younger members seemed a bit reticent, and sometimes I would throw something out to help kick-start the discussion. But ego was the main driver. I was still the little school boy in the second row, waving his hand in the air saying, "I know! Ask me! Ask me!"

As much as I wanted an A+ in RCIA, I also wanted a firm, crystal-clear understanding of Catholic doctrine. Sure, sure, I knew these were all deep, complex matters. Still, Catholics were known for their core beliefs, right? When I joined the Cub Scouts in the second grade, I memorized a pledge, something like: "I promise to do my duty, to God and my country, to help other people, to be square, and to obey the Law of the Pack." I loved saying that pledge every week at pack meetings. My father loved the army and was proud, all things considered, to have been a soldier. I was proud to think that I would be joining an organization like the church. At that point, if they had given me a Catholic uniform, I would have worn it. If they'd told me to go and get a Catholic tattoo, I would have done it. A henna tattoo, at least.

I wanted something very simple that I could hang my hat on. I'd go back later and develop a deeper understanding, but for the moment, I wanted a Cub Scout sort of pledge. I wanted Core Beliefs, church-at-a-glance, something that could fit on a card I could carry in my wallet. I also had the thought, noodling around in the back of my mind, that extremism in defense of the church is no vice. Somewhere inside me was a fundamentalist yearning to breathe free. I could prove just how sincerely I believed by becoming a *True* Believer, by accepting even the simplest statement of faith without any qualms. Michael kept cheerfully deflecting this ambition of mine. He offered me more information, more insights, and more doctrines. But he never gave me The Final Word.

One Sunday in late October we were looking at the Nicene Creed. "This is what I tell folks when they ask what it means to be a Catholic," Michael said.

Ha! I knew he'd been holding back. This was more like it. I'd been saying this creed in church for almost a year. But as I studied it, questions kept popping up, especially about the identity of Christ.

Lauren once told me a story about when she was a receptionist at a law firm in Manhattan. She was talking to one of the partners, a big guy in the entertainment business. She was trying to figure out what exactly it was he did for a living. Finally she said, "You're a mogul, right?"

He was pleased with the term and said, "Yeah, that's me."

Then she asked, "So what's the hardest thing about being a mogul?"

He thought for a moment and said, "People are always trying to unmogul you."

That's what the Nicene Creed is fighting. Part of me was trying to unmogul Christ, just like we sometimes try to unmogul God, unmogul the Spirit, unmogul Mary and all the saints. We want to make Christ simpler and more manageable than he really is. But the Creed reminds us, line after line, that Christ is a supremely unmanageable paradox: not either-or but both-and—both physical and divine, both God and the Son of God, both a man in history and a resurrected figure who transcends time. Naturally we want to dismantle this paradox and reduce it to two easy pieces, or maybe just one. The more I thought about it, the more profound this paradox appeared to me, doing glorious violence to any logical attempts to understand it. Carmen at the Corpus Christi Abbey had been right: Christianity isn't a system; it's a Person, the Person of Christ.

Let me put it another way. A friend of mine teaches Shakespeare in college. He once told me that one of his students kept asking about the "point" of Hamlet. "We know all sorts of things about this character, this prince, but what's the final point? What's the point of Hamlet?"

My friend, inspired, responded with, "What's the point of you? Do you have a point?"

I was realizing that as a person, Christ doesn't have a mere point, a single, simple kernel of truth. And as a part of the body of Christ on earth, the church doesn't have a single point either. As a Christian, I couldn't assume to know what God is thinking. I should simply embrace the paradox and resist reducing everything to a wallet card.

I was getting my head around the idea of "mystery." I saw the word defined somewhere as a religious truth that's hard to understand. Catholics are all over mystery. The sacraments are a mystery. Sin is a mystery. Grace is a mystery. The church itself is a mystery. I began to think of mystery as something like staring into a pool of water that's infinitely deep. The water itself is completely clear. There's nothing murky or fuzzy about a religious mystery. But the light of our reason, as it were, can penetrate only so far, and it isn't apparent even how far that is. Try understanding the Trinity, and at a certain depth, your mind just sort of plays out. You know you understand something to some degree, but there are no hard edges, no clearly defined floor to your understanding.

In the RCIA, I often felt the same way I did while wading along creeks with my boys in the Hill Country. I might walk along the shallows for a while, with the limestone rock visible under the water, but then I would step down into a deep stretch and push off into the water and float, a bit giddy, unable to see bottom. If I wanted paradox, if I wanted both the gridwork and the glow, then here it was, mysteries upon mysteries, and the highest mystery was God. Here was Truth, as well as the richest, most intellectually successful way to approach it that I had ever found.

⌒⌒⌒

In November I finally finished the Bible. Every single word, every jot and tittle. I was whipped. I'd been getting up before the chickens for a year now. Also, the initial adrenaline rush of beginning the RCIA had died down. As much as I still wanted to join the church, I was all Bibled out, churched out, Massed out. A priest had told me that "faith means seeing through things." I liked that. I could understand how "through" could mean both "beyond" and "by means of" the physical world. Everything on earth is charged with a sacramental meaning. But seeing through things was exactly what I was losing. I didn't get all misty-eyed during Mass anymore. Instead, I caught a cold from the boys, and both my ears got plugged up. "You're still trying not to hear something," said Lauren, who always saw illness in symbolic terms. All I knew was that I was beat. My faith was still there, but it was burning with a low, blue flame.

I tried to schedule some time off. I wasn't sure if I had calculated my vacation days correctly, but I claimed them all anyway. I asked for two weeks around Christmas. The Boss replied with a flaming e-mail. (Our offices were side by side but we usually communicated online.) "You know how much you have to do regarding our current public relations campaign as well as our spring show. How do you propose to satisfy your duties here while taking off two full weeks? In addition, your days requested don't match my estimates." (She'd gone back and rechecked the calendar over the past twelve months.) "Richard, I shouldn't have to manage every detail regarding your duties at this company!"

Sigh. Okay, Okay, I was trying to sneak one by her. It reminded me of a billboard I spotted on the freeway:

I saw that.
—God

But if God was keeping me honest, he was also helping me keep in mind why I was entering the church. I decided to go to the Thanksgiving service, and it turned out to be one of the best Masses all year. As Father P.J. said, Thanksgiving is a holy day of obligation that's not a day of obligation. Everyone who showed up was there because they wanted to be there. Our response throughout the Liturgy of the Word was strong and vibrant. We almost scared ourselves. Then it was time to present our gifts. We had all been asked to bring shopping bags of food for those who were hungry. When Father asked us to bring our gifts forward, the church was filled with the rolling thunder of five hundred paper and plastic bags crinkling and rustling as they were lifted and carried. As I stood up with my own bag of canned goods, I looked across the church and thought, *This is the Kingdom of God. It's where you say, "Here. Take this. Take everything. It's yours." It's where you give and give and give until at last you're free.* For a moment then, I think I got it, if only a glimpse.

After Thanksgiving I was still tired, and I could feel myself slumping into my usual Christmas depression. When I was a child, I was always naturally delighted with Christmas. But after turning twelve, I started dreading it for the usual reasons: the way it's been taken over by consumerism, all the phoniness of official holiday cheer. Like a lot of people, I was angry at Christmas precisely because I loved it. I wanted to recover that O-Little-Town-of-Bethlehem feeling that I once shared with my mother as we set out the candles and arranged the angel hair on the mantelpiece. Christmas was one of the few times she and I got along.

I talked with Jean, a Catholic spiritual director, who gave me several pieces of good advice, but I remember one in particular. "Think about Our Lady," she said. "You especially."

Why me especially? Did that make any sense?

"Oh yeah. Big time," said Lauren when I told her later about Jean's advice. As a Protestant boy, I had never really thought about Mary.

I said, "There's a date coming up—"

"December eighth."

"Right. The feast of the Immaculate Conception. Maybe I'll go to that. Of course, you might pooh-pooh that idea, being lapsed and all."

"Hey, buddy, don't dismiss me and the church," she said. I was surprised at her tone. She added, "We go back a long way, thank you very much. I'd like to think my relationship is just as complex as yours. Remember, I was praying to Our Lady way back in New York when you couldn't be bothered, when we were first trying to get pregnant. And remember going to San Antonio?"

"I remember going there for Spencer."

"No, we went twice. Honey, where's your memory? We'd been trying to get pregnant all those years . . ."

"Four."

"Yes, and nothing was working. And I went to that awful fertility clinic where the receptionist had a diamond ring that was worth more than our entire apartment, and the waiting room was filled with women sobbing and writing out checks."

"Where was I?"

"Oh, out of town on business. And we decided not to go with the clinic, and about that time someone told me about St. Thérèse of Lisieux, how she was very practical. When she died, she told everyone she was going to heaven to answer people's prayers. Pray to the Little Flower for something specific, and you'll get something specific in return. So you went to the Village and bought a portrait of St. Thérèse, and we put it up in our kitchen. Then a few weeks later we went to Austin, and we drove down to San Antonio with Sulinda and James. It was incredibly cold. Maybe ten degrees."

"Right. We almost froze."

"And we went to those mission churches along the river, and as we were going from one to the other I realized that, no, we weren't visiting museums; we were on a pilgrimage. So I started praying, and in one of the chapels I was given a message that I was going to have a son."

"Yeah, I remember, and then, bingo! You got pregnant the week we got back from Texas."

"You were very impressed," she said.

"Well, yes, after four years of trying."

"But you still had doubts. And I had to remind you that the mission church was named Concepción."

"Ah. Yes." Little flashes of providence I had tried to ignore. Trying to convince Lauren that I hadn't totally blanked on the year, I said, "I do remember when you told me you were pregnant. We were in that shop in Chinatown, the one that sold herbal medicines."

"Linn's Sister on Elizabeth Street. I loved that address!"

"We'd been buying these Chinese fertility pills. They weren't working, but we were buying them anyway, and I asked if we needed some more, and you said, 'I don't think so.' You were very casual, but that moment is seared into my brain."

"Good. Mine, too."

"And afterward we went to a tea shop, and you told me you were probably pregnant. I remember that while you were telling me this, I was watching a couple behind you at a table in the window. He looked like a Chinese gangster, and she looked like his—what would you call her—his moll? They were something out of a movie. It was surreal, very New York. But they looked so bored, bored with each other, and I was thinking here we were, entering a whole new chapter in our life."

"And then after Harrison was born," she added, "we got pregnant the second time, and we had the miscarriage."

That I remember—clearly. Lauren had been feeling fine during the second pregnancy, but we were worried. With Harrison, she was nauseated day and night. It was a sign that the pregnancy was "taking." In my mind, her pregnancies will always be associated with a very distinctive, three-part "cough-cough-gag" sound coming from the bathroom. I heard that for months. But with this pregnancy, she had only a trace of nausea. We crossed our fingers. Then at eighteen weeks, she started bleeding. At first, we hoped it was something else, but after two more days she started bleeding heavily. We called our midwife, who told us to get to a hospital fast. I called a car service, we parked Harrison at our neighbor's home, and Lauren and I went to Beth Israel in Manhattan. She was admitted to the ER, and I sat in the lobby, watching PBS on the TV. Two hours later, the doctors let me see her. We'd lost the baby.

That punched a big hole in both of us. We went through real grieving, more than we expected, and it lasted for weeks and months. We still talk about it, still think about that baby, whether it would have been a boy or a girl, what that child would be doing now if it had survived.

Lauren continued, "Then I got pregnant again, and we went to San Antonio a second time, remember? It was during the summer, July, after you'd been laid off, and we were thinking about moving to Austin. It was like a hundred degrees this time."

"Right, and you were bleeding again."

"Yes, just like before, and I didn't feel particularly nauseated, and both of us were very depressed. We thought we were going to lose this one too. You'd been wanting to go to the mission for years to give thanks for Harrison. I was the one who said Our Lady would understand if we didn't visit her, but you insisted. So when we got to Austin, you told your sister you wanted to go to San Antonio so we could visit the mission, and we decided to go down there with Sulinda and all the kids and go to SeaWorld at the same time."

"You bought red roses to give to Our Lady."

"Actually, you bought the roses, sweetie," she said. "You were a Catholic even then; you just didn't know it. So we went to all the mission churches, but we couldn't find La Concepción. The kids were getting cranky because they were hot and wanted to get to SeaWorld. I kept bleeding, and we were getting more depressed. So we finally said we'd just go to one more mission, and that turned out to be San José.

Sulinda stayed with the kids in the SUV with the air conditioning going and all the kids whining, and you and I went inside the church and found an absolutely beautiful Lady chapel. And that's when we had our vision."

"I don't remember any vision. I just remember the chapel was incredibly bright."

"Well, I think we both had visions. We kinda wandered back to the car, and we all went out to lunch, and that's when I suddenly got really, really sick. And I went to the bathroom and found I'd stopped bleeding. It was like twenty minutes after we'd been to the chapel."

"You looked white. I felt bad for you."

"Well, I was miserable. Then I had to tromp around SeaWorld in that awful heat for hours, feeling like I was going to throw up any minute. But I was overjoyed because I knew what had happened."

So Lauren was right. Both pregnancies were involved with Our Lady and the mission churches. I told her I'd talk to Our Lady on the eighth.

I went to the 5:30 Mass at St. Austin. Forty years ago I'd read *The Old Man and the Sea* and memorized the Hail Mary from it. For decades it was the only prayer, certainly the only Catholic prayer, I knew by heart. Mary seemed to have an odd power, profound but not overt. More yin than yang. She might not be up there in the Trinity, but that was part and parcel with her yin role, and yin balanced the yang in the universe. Christ himself embraced this yin role. He wasn't a yang general or the yang messiah the Jews expected but the Prince of Peace, very yin, who conquered the world, as yin always does eventually.

I sat through the homily thinking about yin giving birth to yang who conveyed the strength of yin until my head got dizzy. After Mass I went over to the Lady chapel and sat for a while. You can't ignore Mom, and she never ignores you. Even with my own mother and all the problems we had, I never believed that she didn't love me. Intensely disappointed with me at times. Infuriated, yes. But she was always fiercely loyal to both her children.

I sat there for a few minutes with my eyes closed, listening as the crowd slowly filtered out of the church. And then I started crying, longer and harder than I had for months, my face buried in my hands. I wasn't sad or even upset. I just felt like my heart was going to bust. After several minutes I sputtered to a stop, exhausted but peaceful. I took a deep breath, pulled myself together, got up, bowed to the statue of Mary, and walked out of the church.

I dropped into my car and drove home. When I told Lauren about the Mass and about crying in the chapel, she nodded and said, "Like your heart was going to bust, right?"

"Yes, actually," I said, and once again I was grateful to be married to someone who understood something of what I was going through, who didn't think this conversion was silly or neurotic but a natural part of life. She had been there.

That Christmas was better than I ever expected. It wasn't a secular holiday anymore. It was Advent, and the days now had a wistful, beautiful sadness to them. It was the time of Mary, with child. Yes, the holiday had its ups and downs. We had to go to company parties. The boys squabbled over their toys. We were broke at the end of the year. But this wasn't "Xmas" anymore. This was Advent, and by the liturgical calendar, it was the beginning, not the end, of the year. I now had a new sense of the year's cycles, a new sense of time, and for the first time since I was twelve, I was at peace with the season.

9

Radio Astronomy

I tell you by the eternal truth that so long as you desire to fulfill the will of God and have any hankering after eternity and God, for just so long you are not truly poor. He alone has true spiritual poverty who wills nothing, knows nothing, desires nothing.

—Meister Eckhart

Lauren and I have this running joke about the "Rule of Two." If we go to a new restaurant or take the kids to a park and everybody has a great time, we naturally want to repeat the experience. But when we go back, it's just not as good. I think it's because we're trying too hard, trying to engineer the event. We usually have to go back a third time, without any expectations, to break through the Rule.

In January I decided to go back to the abbey. Maybe the Rule of Two wouldn't apply to monasteries. I'd been on my new path for a year. I wanted to go back to the community where it all started. It would be an opportunity to take stock, to see if I'd changed; and maybe I'd get more insight. Look what happened the first time I went! Maybe God would suspend the rules. He could, of course.

When I arrived at the abbey, everything looked the same: small and tired. I gave the porter at the front door my name.

"Oh yes, we remember you," he said. "We've been praying for you."

What did that mean? I didn't want to ask. I thanked him and walked over to the retreat center. My room was the one I'd had before, in St. Meinrad Hall. I had already made an appointment with

Carmen, so I walked over to the retreat office. She showed up right on time. We sat down in the lobby of the retreat center, face-to-face, our chairs close together, the way you sometimes do these days in confession. Nobody was around, and the grounds were completely quiet. Carmen smiled, waiting for me to begin. I took a breath, then dropped my bombshell: I was converting to Catholicism. I had entered the RCIA.

She nodded pleasantly.

I paused. That's it? A nod? I'd just told her about one of the biggest events of my life! God had spoken! And spoken to me! I wanted congratulations. Expressions of joy and surprise. High fives.

Nothing. She waited for me to continue. So I filled her in with what I'd been trying to do spiritually over the past year—all the reading, the thinking, the self-assessment. All the while, I was thinking about Moses coming down from Sinai with the light of God in his face. His people couldn't even look at him, his face was so bright. So was my face shining? Huh? Huh?

Carmen waited until I'd rolled to a stop. "It sounds as if you've been very busy," she said.

"Actually, I feel as if I've been wasting my time all these years, so maybe now I'm playing catch-up."

"Don't worry about wasting time. In fact, I'd say waste your time while you're here."

"Waste time?"

"Yes, my direction to you for your stay here is—no direction. Just listen. That is, feel, taste, sense what's around you."

I was furiously writing all this down in my notebook.

She waited until I'd stopped, then continued, "God has brought you here for a reason. So just wait. Something will happen. Go down to the wharf. Feel the wind on your cheek. Wait. Don't worry about whether you accomplish something or not."

As she talked, a tape was running in my head. "If you waste time, you run out of time. If you run out of time, you're dead." I tried to focus on what she was saying.

She continued, "God talks to us in moods, dreams, memories, impulses, images. So just open yourself to these things. Just listen."

I thanked her and went back to my little motel room in St. Meinrad Hall and lay on the bed. That was it? Just be-here-now for three days? Just listen? That would be difficult. Expect nothing, as Simone Weil once said. But I didn't bring Weil's book this time, or anything else to read and study this time. Just a notebook and a Bible.

That night, as with the first time I went to the abbey, I couldn't sleep. The room seemed stuffy, and the mattress sagged in the middle. I kept turning and checking my glow-in-the-dark travel clock. Around midnight I got up, got dressed, and wandered out to the church.

A few weeks before in an RCIA class, one of the candidates mentioned she was going to a retreat community south of Corpus Christi for the New Year. She admitted that she was probably overpreparing for the event, bringing along several Bibles and the *Spiritual Exercises* of St. Ignatius. So how should she pray? Discursive prayers? Centering? Mantras? What?

Michael gave her that smile of his and suggested that she might try leaving all her books at home. "I just want to suggest something," he said. "Dance with God. Don't read or study. Just try dancing, literally dancing with the Lord."

With that in mind I walked to the front of the church and the statue of Jesus. His arms reached out to me in the darkness. I looked around. Then I slowly began to dance, kind of freestyle, twirling around, rising and falling, my arms in the air. I felt the same way I had the first time I knelt in front of the grotto of Our Lady of Guadalupe. I was "incriminating" myself. I was trying to dance with God.

I'd like to say that somewhere in the dancing, music welled up inside me and carried me away. But nothing happened. No shining face, no instant spiritual high. After a while I stopped and stood for a minute, listening. Nothing. Only an outboard motor somewhere far across the lake. Was this the Rule of Two? Was I expecting too much?

I went back to bed. Every hour I woke up. Carmen said I was here for a reason, so what was it? Had I made a mistake even to come here? I'd been marching along my Catholic path for a year now. I could follow the Mass; I had a vague notion of Christian theology and the Bible. But had I changed? Could I say that I truly loved God? A TV evangelist in my head kept shouting at me, "Do you accept Jesus-Christ-as-your-personal-Lord-and-Savior? Huh? Do you?" Yes, I said. But did I really? No. I mean, yes! Well, yes . . . in a way. Some days, every word I read in the Bible rang with truth, and I embraced it totally. "I am the way, the truth, and the life." Of course! But other days, the gray days when I was tired and skeptical, everything I read seemed to have quotes around it—"I" "am" "the" "way," as if I could accept those words only in a philosophical, even ironic sense, as if Christ were simply a literary metaphor.

But now wasn't the time to be literary, and it wasn't the time to be intellectually fastidious in my doubts. I'd tried doubt for almost half a century. Screw doubt. Believe me, doubt went nowhere. Now was the time to fully embrace the literal fact that God loved me. So why did I keep resisting that fact? Inside me a little voice kept whimpering, "I don't deserve your love," but that sounded bogus. It was sandbagging. Yeats said that "in dreams begins responsibility," and the same goes for love. Accepting someone's love means being responsible in and for a relationship. But maybe I wasn't ready for a relationship with God. Better to just think about God, a part of me said. Better to just feel something about God than to be with God himself. Better to stay in my study and read. Better to dance by myself.

Saturday

Doing nothing is hard, of course, especially if you're on deadline. I had two days. I got up before dawn   still couldn't sleep—and went down to the retreat center's kitchenette to make a cup of coffee. The little kitchen hadn't been cleaned in what looked like weeks. The sink was filled with old dishes, and there were three or four coffee machines on the counter, none of them clean. I turned on the faucet to clean one of them. The plumbing shuddered and a little water dribbled out, then a burst shot out and splattered me. I toweled my face off with some coffee filters and went into the dining room looking for another faucet.

The dining room was large and dark, filled with long tables. For some reason, all the tables were covered with clean table cloths, a centerpiece of plastic flowers on each table, with salt and pepper shakers and little caddies of sugar packets. It looked as if a large crowd were going to come through the doors any second. As far as I knew, I was the only person at the center. Maybe the monks had expectations.

In the back kitchen I found a faucet that worked, filled my mug, went back to the kitchenette and heated up the water and instant coffee in the microwave. Ah, what we do for drugs.

After morning prayers and Mass, I bounced around the abbey grounds, trying to listen, to feel, to be in the moment, etc., etc. It was tough slugging. *Waste time. Waste time*, I told myself, looking at my watch. I walked down to the lake and sat on the pier.

I closed my eyes and sat very still, listening to the birds. Inside, my engine was still revving, thinking about problems, solutions, progress, measurement, getting there, being here, doing. Doing what? Doing something. Anything. Think! Think harder! Salvation is for those who try! Even St. Paul talks about running the race. Winning the prize. God isn't for losers.

I opened my eyes and slapped myself on the cheek. Get a grip, Richard.

At lunch with the brothers I casually mentioned that I was in the RCIA now. I waited for congratulations but everyone just nodded, like Carmen. Over his macaroni and cheese, one of the brothers asked, "Have you seen the library? You might find that useful."

After lunch I went to the library. I hadn't seen this part of the abbey before. It wasn't huge, but it contained a goodly number of books, almost all of them from the forties, fifties, and sixties. I found an old missal from the fifties, a thick, black book bound in leather, about the size and weight of half a brick. I looked through its pages. Everything was spelled out. It reminded me of the *Baltimore Catechism*, like the Latin Masses I went to. The old Catholicism could be a confining world, but you certainly knew your place in it.

This was clearly a working library. Everything was orderly and well arranged. I felt calm and happy here, the way I do in any workshop. I wandered over to the corner. An old Royal typewriter was set on a small table. On it was a note written in ink by hand in an elegant, medieval-looking calligraphy:

> Please do not use or try to adjust any part of this typewriter. It is not only an antique but was used by Abbot Luke Buergler, O.S.B., for much of his work as teacher, priest, prior, retreat master and abbot. In a real sense, it is a sacred relic. Thank you.

Beside the card was a small piece of paper with the Apostles' Creed typed straight out. No typos.

Poking around the library, I learned that the monks had founded a Catholic school for boys, Corpus Christi College-Academy, in 1928. For the next four decades they educated hundreds of boys, and later girls, from South Texas. I looked through the yearbooks at pictures of presiding bishops in frilly lace and horn-rimmed glasses, priests saying Mass for boys in blue jeans with crew cuts. This was an earlier Texas, the one I remembered as a very young child from Krum. I looked through the senior-class section, with the usual school annual questions under each student's picture. Most prized possession: "My boots." Lifetime ambition: "To go to college." Several students said their ambition was to be a rancher. And a few said, "Live a good Catholic life." For years the academy was one of the largest Catholic schools in the state. The monks had been busy. Four priests had come out of that school. Brother James had told me about the old days when they conducted nationwide fund-raising, mailing out over a million envelopes, working for days until midnight.

In 1970, Hurricane Celia damaged several buildings. The monks tried to rebuild, but it was impossible without raising tuition higher than the students could pay. The monks decided to move inland and set up a retreat community. I found a photo album on a back shelf with snapshots from the early days at the lake. It looked like a healthy and vibrant community back then, with lots of volunteers and neat, well-watered lawns. The buildings were newly painted, with confident-looking monks surrounded by student groups. Carmen had told me that it was once very popular with Catholic schools all over the state. It looked like a fresh start for the community.

Then the pictures stopped. A number of the monks had died in the nineties, including most of the priests. I'd seen their names at the mausoleum outside overlooking the lake. Other things apparently happened as well: changes in leadership, maybe just the gradual effects of old age. The large groups of students stopped showing up. The community was still viable these days, but for how long? It needed more money than it obviously had, and it also needed new members to survive. I thought of a small sign at the gates of the abbey—"Fresh Roses." Oh, Lord. How could you support a community by selling flowers in the middle of nowhere?

After dinner I went back to the library. At night, with the reading lamps turned on, everything appeared cozier. I found a folder on retreats and looked through the material: how to run a retreat, what retreatants might be expecting, questions to ask. On the back of a schedule, someone, maybe one of the retreat directors, had written notes in pencil. Were these quotes? Thoughts from one of the monks? One said:

> He who dares to believe reaches a sphere of created reality in which things, while retaining their habitual texture, seem to be made of a different substance. Everything becomes luminous, animated, loving.

I thought of the brothers I'd seen that night, eating their macaroni and cheese in silence. Did they live in a luminous world? I found several other notes about the contemplative life, the power of prayer and faith. One note was written in another hand:

> I can still see only one answer: to keep pressing on, in ever-increasing faith. MAY THE RISEN CHRIST KEEP ME YOUNG! Which means optimistic, active, clear-sighted and happy.

As I read, I began to have a sharp feeling of shame. The brothers who had written these thoughts were the Christians I'd called the schlumps of God. Who did I think I was? How could I even begin to assess their devotion and what they had accomplished? Yes, the community was tired. Okay, downright shabby. But God had sent them here to the lake for a reason, just like me, and maybe they were doing exactly what God wanted them to do, and doing it well, whether I could understand that or not.

I put away the folder. Had I made enough "progress" for the day? I mean, other than realizing what an ignorant little snot I was? I turned off the lights and walked back to the front door. As I passed the porter, I saw two monks, making a little joke about the roast beef they had last Sunday. One of them had been the cook. Gentle teasing between them. *What dear men*, I thought. I said good night to the porter who was listening to his radio, and I stepped out into the darkness.

I walked back under the stars. A full moon was rising in the east, and the lake was shining. I thought about the monks. Perhaps they weren't leading special lives but rather ordinary lives in a special way.

Later that night, brushing my teeth, I started thinking about radio astronomy. Maybe the monks were like radio astronomers. Why not? Perhaps their life out here was a kind of listening, for themselves and also for all of us who were too dazzled or distracted or puffed up with pride or choked with anger or grief to hear what God was trying to tell us. I imagined the abbey grounds dotted with those big satellite dishes that radio astronomers use, silently, patiently tracking the heavens prayer by prayer and day by day. Along with whatever else the monks might be doing, maybe they're simply listening. Listening is a kind of poverty, making yourself empty so you can better receive. Maybe that's why they were in the middle of nowhere, away from all the noise and blare. This abbey was a kind of observatory, and perhaps on this isolated bluff, the monks could better hear those small, still voices, those faint signals from somewhere on the other side of the galaxy inside our hearts.

Sunday

During Sunday Mass, my mood began to change—odd how that works—and somehow the day seemed brighter and calmer. The congregation was a mixture of the monks and neighbors in the area, mainly ranchers and people living around the lake, many of them in their sixties or older. I sat in the back and watched the others receive communion. In a few months, perhaps, I'd be up at the altar myself.

I had an appointment to talk to Carmen after lunch. In the meantime, I went over to the gift shop to look around. Catholics have great gear; I'd always admired their medals, cards, crosses, statues, and whatnot. The shop was smaller than I expected, the shelves almost bare, but the monk was friendly, a small man with gray, close-cropped hair. He was interested in why I'd come to the monastery, and he seemed to brighten when I told him I was joining the church. He recommended a St. Benedict medal. "Very, very powerful, actually," he said in a guarded tone. "When we were in Corpus Christi, somebody opened one of those X-rated video stores, you know."

"Yes."

"And it was right across the street from the school, right there in front of the boys! I couldn't stand it, so one night I took a St. Benedict's medal and threw it over the roof. Six months later, the store closed."

"Wow."

"Oh yes," he nodded, his eyes widening, and just for a moment I thought I saw a very old Catholicism, the kind that bordered on a belief in the magical. It was spooky in a compelling sort of way. I thanked him and paid for the medal and a chain.

As I turned to leave, he reached under the counter and offered me a small, brown Benedictine crucifix. "Here. Take this. And please, pray for us."

"Is everything all right?" I asked.

"Yes, but we need your prayers. We have a visitation from our mother abbey coming up. Every community has to be self-supporting, and if we can't show that we can take care of ourselves, we'll have to move."

For a moment, he looked very small and vulnerable, holding the crucifix out to me, and I realized that he was talking about one of the greatest fears of any of us who are growing old: losing our home and having to move to a strange place and be cared for by strangers. This abbey might not be large, but it was where they expected to die, surrounded by their brothers who were their best friends and true family. Instead of peacefully living out their lives here, they might someday, as Christ said to Peter, have to stretch out their hands, and someone else would dress them, and lead them where they did not want to go. I accepted the crucifix, and I told him, yes, I would pray. Of course. He stood by the door, smiling again as I left the shop.

"Don't analyze," Carmen said when we sat down. "Think about what's happened to you this weekend, but don't analyze it. You don't evaluate a loving relationship. You're simply there with the beloved."

I closed my notebook. She added, "One more thing: God wants to you be happy. Jesus, or saints like St. John of the Cross, they all knew pain—a great deal of it—and yet they wanted us to be happy. I'm not talking about being what you might call pathologically nice. Simply accept the happiness that God gives us."

"Ah." I couldn't think of anything to say, so I didn't say anything.

She continued, "The true leaders in this world aren't the politicians or rulers or millionaires. They're the people who are truly happy. We all naturally gravitate to these people. We try to shape our lives around what they represent because we realize that what they have is more powerful than anything. So be happy. Life should be something like a festival."

She was sounding like Father Norm the Episcopalian! Another example of God's sense of humor. We talked a bit more; then I thanked her and asked if I could write to her from time to time. She wrote down her name and mailing address, and I asked about her last name. And where did that accent come from?

"It's Basque," she said. "My name means Wide Truth," and she smiled as if sharing a joke.

We said good-bye, and she gave me a big hug, an *abrazo*. Everyone seemed much friendlier this time around. Were they changing? Was I?

She said, "Think of the abbey as your home away from home." As I went out the door, she called out, "Remember, God is crazy about you!"

❦

Carmen told me not to analyze, so, of course, I chewed things over all the way back to Austin. For the past three days I'd been looking for Significance. Every event, every remark might be a message in a bottle. Carmen said that God brought me there for a reason, but she didn't say I'd ever know why.

Over the next few weeks, however, I began to understand at least why I wanted to go. To be honest, I went there looking for a place to hide. I had the notion that a monastery was a refuge, a way to escape your problems. God knows I'd been looking for escapes all my life—in books, in bottles, inside my head. I also went there looking for someone to take care of me. And I wanted clear answers, about my path, how far I'd come, and about what God had in store for me. In all these expectations, the abbey was a complete bust, and that was its blessing. I realized that if the community had been a prosperous, well-oiled operation, I might have actually been intimidated. Or I might have come away with confusion about material success and spiritual value, as if one was proof of the other. Or I might have thought I had more answers than I really did because the community was exactly what I expected. But expectations were part of the baggage the pilgrim had to abandon on his quest, right?

As it was, the community was more like a friendship. It had something to offer, but also something to ask of me, if only patience and a bit of understanding. I was more like the monks than I had wanted to believe. I had gone there feeling old and less than successful, and that was exactly what I had found: myself as an abbey, myself as the monks. Their thin voices were mine as I sang in the stalls, and that was the greatest gift they gave me, a brotherhood I didn't even recognize at the time.

I had been blessed simply by being in their presence. On my last day I kept trying to think of a way to thank the community. When I gave the porter my check on the way out, he wished me a safe trip, and I wanted to say something about the community and radio astronomy and listening. But no. If someone gives you a gift, you say thank you, so that's what I did. I told him that the community had helped me enormously, that the monks were doing important work.

He seemed to be touched by what I said, this elderly monk, and his kind eyes looked even kinder for a moment. "Thanks," he said. "We don't often hear that."

10

Learning to Die

The false self must die—with Christ on the cross. . . . Then the true inner self, the self animated by the renewing Spirit, can emerge with Christ from the tomb. This is the Paschal mystery that is at the heart of all that is Christian and truly human. It is not enough to remain the same self, the same individual ego, taking on a new set of activities and a lot of religious practices, no matter how good.

—Basil M. Pennington

[Jesus said,] "Let the dead bury their dead."

—Matthew 8:22

It sounds so melodramatic, dying for Christ. I mean, you don't *really* die. That's only a metaphor, right? You keep breathing. The world goes on. You don't ever totally flip out, and actually that's very healthy. Trying to embrace the love of God could lead to psychosis, to ego disintegration, right? "If we want to be holy," said Thomas Merton, "let us first lead our ordinary lives."

But Christ never talked in half measures. Merton also wrote, "In order to find myself I must go out of myself, in order to live I must die." Over and over, Christ tells that we can never find him in a more-or-less fashion. As gradual as our path might be, it's finally all or nothing. You can't fudge God.

Yes, yes. I knew that. Ye must be born again. *Grumble.* I looked at the calendar. The middle of January. Lent would begin next month.

Then we would have forty days, forty-eight with Sundays thrown in, and then Easter. We were moving into the home stretch.

If only I could have one of those near-death experiences right about now, a real clincher, like St. Paul on the road to Damascus. Now *there* was a conversion experience you could bank on: a stunning vision with light and Christ's voice. Then groping blind in the dust and being led, still blind, into the next town, where your sight is miraculously restored. You're born again, and you lead a radically different life with a new name and a new job. A part of me was envious. You could go on a talk show with a story like that.

I didn't see any blinding light in the cards for me. My way seemed more like a long winnowing process. If the false self, the false ego, had to die, then I had to find the damn thing first.

I decided to start with something simple, like coffee. Every morning I still got drunk on caffeine. Without it, all my agendas collapsed. When it was introduced to England in the seventeenth century, coffee was called the "opium of the Puritans." To tea-sipping moderates at the time, those coffee-drinking Puritans showed an unnatural, even alarming intensity. The black hats seemed to take their faith a bit too seriously, the same way they took their work too seriously. No wonder coffee became America's national beverage. It's a way to cement our egos and give us a reassuringly vivid sense of self. After three or four cups of fresh ego-cement, I felt elevated and slightly manic with the feel of my own intelligence. Drink enough coffee, and everything was poetry. But was I looking at the world more clearly or just reveling in self-awareness at the very time I was trying to shuck the ego and all its limitations?

I'm not trying to make this caffeine habit more important than it was. It's not as if I was popping amphetamines. But coffee seemed to represent yet another way I was still holding on to ego.

Caffeine could also open the door to anger, one of my drugs of choice. One Sunday morning I made the mistake of having a double espresso an hour before Mass. Lauren, the boys, and I filed into church. I was tense and anxious. I could feel my jaw clinching and the cords standing out on my neck. I started obsessing about whether Harrison was saying the words correctly. Walking down the aisle to receive our blessings, I almost stumbled over him as I made sure that he had his arms crossed properly as we approached the altar.

We both received the priest's blessings and returned to our seats. We looked at each other. "Whew," I said. "We made it!" He snuggled against me, resting his head on my shoulder, and finally I felt at peace. I held him close and watched the rest of the congregation receive communion. I saw that both the ministers giving out the communion and the people receiving it looked as though it was Christmas morning, as if this communion was the greatest gift in the world, as if they'd momentarily forgotten who or where they were. This was what the liturgy was about. It was holy gift-giving. The more I could focus on that gift, that blessing, instead of on getting it "right," the closer I could be to what God was trying to give me.

Maybe I could give up coffee for Lent, though I had my doubts.

Every morning the voice said, "You must die." And every morning, I thought, yes, but how? How does the false self die? Do I just throw myself on the floor? Hold my breath till I pass out? If I need to step over a cliff into thin air, where's the cliff? Where's the air?

Maybe the cliff was all around me. I noticed that I was using the word "secular" a lot in describing American popular culture. Like most Americans, I had grown up both entertained and ironic when it came to the media. I had even helped create it, working for years in advertising. But now it seemed that I was looking at TV commercials, print ads, and even the products themselves through the wrong end of a telescope. The words and images I'd been swimming in for years now seemed way too focused on speed, power, control, wealth, and all those other things that amplify our sense of self. Madalyn Murray O'Hair (herself an Austinite) used to complain bitterly about how Christian values were imposed on the American public. But now I realized that much of American culture wasn't Christian at all.

To some folks, this is hardly news, but it was a revelation for me. The values of American consumerism promised a kind of salvation I couldn't accept anymore, even in an ironic way. I remember a billboard that I passed every morning on my way to work. I can't recall what it was advertising, but the headline said, "Feel the Power. Yield to None."

"Well, no," I told myself. "You don't live like that. You yield to God. He has the power; we don't." I would watch TV and surf through the blur of sex and violence with a growing sense that something was wrong with these pictures. Granted, my wife and I and the boys had been living in Mr. Rogers' Neighborhood for the past decade, and maybe I was just showing my age, but I found myself edging away from entire continents of popular culture. Robert Bly (odd how he kept popping up in my life) once said that American values are great—until you hit age thirty-five or so. Then they start to be inadequate for what life demands, and I agreed. I didn't expect any longer to go to my grave feeling the power and yielding to none.

If I chose a Christian path leading away from this culture, I'd also have to accept the possibility of becoming somebody's target. A lot of people saw religion as the problem, not the solution. I started noticing, really noticing for the first time, bumper stickers in Austin that said:

Don't Pray in My School, and I Won't Think in Your Church

or

Freedom of Religion Is Freedom *from* Religion

or

My God Is Too Big for Your Church

No, your ego *is too big for my church*. But it hurt to see those words. I used to think like that myself, of course, and not too long ago. But now those attitudes seemed unthinking and self-righteous. The bumper stickers opposed to all religion even seemed a bit quaint, an archaic leftover from the twentieth century, modernism, and an unquestioning faith in science. That was fine as far as it went, but secular materialism just couldn't substitute for what I was finding now. Perhaps the next century would be a new age of faith.

Something, a tiny something, was definitely changing inside me. Not that I was wandering through the streets in a hair shirt, moaning. Every morning I got up, took my vitamins, went to work, came home, helped Harrison with his homework, and watched TV. I was Joe Normal. But I found myself in unexpected places. I was beginning to say words I'd never used much before, such as *redemption, atonement, sin, salvation*. They felt odd, like marbles in my mouth.

I still kept hearing the voice telling me that I had to die, to reject my false self. So I tried to unpack that self and reassess all those glittering, useless elements I thought I needed.

For decades, poetry had been at the center of my life, but I hadn't written anything in years, and Lauren, supportive as she'd been, was much happier when I stopped. "It's like having a husband back," she said. "You have so much more energy for us when you're not always racing off to your study to write." Well, yes, fair enough. If God wanted me to write poetry or anything else, I'd follow his direction. But if he never wanted me to write anything at all for the rest of my life, well, so be it. If that sounds like heroic self-denial, then let me also tell you that a big part of me was greatly relieved not to write. I'd been driving on fumes for a long time. Inside, my creativity was exhausted. I'd rather pray and read.

And what about intellectual pride? That was a long-standing attitude, hard to kick. I remember going to the library with my mother when I was a child. I would always check out a big stack of books on Science and Other Important Stuff. I remember looking down my little nose at other people who were checking out silly books like mystery novels. Reading for pleasure! Harrumph. They weren't doing really serious reading like me. I must have been all of seven.

That child was still inside me, of course. So I tried to keep in mind how little I knew about the Bible, theology, Catholicism, anything at all. How Christ said that his message was for the children and the simple folk, and that he didn't choose his disciples for their education or whether or not they had made A's. In fact, learning could be an obstacle if you stopped at that.

What else? I dug a bit deeper. Ah, vanity—that beautiful face staring up from the reflecting pond, and while we're at it, let's make that sexual vanity. I had always prided myself on being the understanding male. Other men might be big-shouldered brutes who just wanted to get laid. I was nobler. I had always been interested in what my lovers had to say and how they looked at the world. Listening to someone made me more attractive to her—I'd known that all along. Yes, I truly had been interested, but I had used this show of interest in getting exactly what I wanted.

There's more. One night, Lauren and I were watching a movie, *As Good as It Gets*, while the kids were watching their own entertainment in the front room. At one point, the Helen Hunt character asks a young man in for a drink at the end of the evening.

Like many people, I had always thought of myself as attractive. I still made eye contact with other women every now and then, and sometimes I saw (or thought I saw) a brief, flickering connection as we passed each other. It gave me a pleasant ego-squeeze to know that I still had it, even though "it" was fast fading with age. Now I was watching this scene where the young man tried to—is *seduce* still a word?—tried to arouse, to become sexual with the Helen Hunt character, and he started slowly licking her face. It was a painful farce. She was cringing, and I started cringing as well because that young man was myself at that age.

I remembered all those years when I thought I was a special gift to women. I tried to make them feel beautiful, but that was only when I wasn't being a jerk. Watching the movie, I could see that blind arrogance and sexual pride would have to be another layer of the onion to peel away.

I looked at my watch. Three weeks until Lent. I knew I was avoiding something. What was at the core of this false self? Anger? Check. Self-pity? Check. Pride? Oh yeah, pride's a good one. Everything stems from pride. But really, what was I missing? What truly would be the most difficult thing for me to give up?

In my conversations with Michael, he had asked me to think about what I feared the most and how God could help me face that fear. My first reaction was that I didn't have any major fears at this point in my life. (What was I thinking?) But as I walked around with the question, I remembered the fears that had helped shepherd me—and cattle prod me—into wanting to join the church. The biggest one, even bigger than dying, was being perceived as a loser.

You can call Americans a lot of things, but you never, ever, ever call us losers. Being a loser is a secular curse, the ultimate middle-class damnation. We're here on earth to win. Money is how you keep score, said the tycoon. The game of football is like the game of life, said my high school principal. Most of us find out eventually that life isn't a game at all, but the idea can be appealing, as if everything could be as simple as a game, with rule books, teams, uniforms, and a final, undeniable victory at the end of play.

All through my life, even when I was working in the liquor store with my almost Ph.D., I felt that I was still some sort of winner. If I wasn't a corporate vice president or a successful entrepreneur like my father, well, that was fine. I would be judged by a more refined measure—as an artist, not as a businessman. But as the years went by and the writing career sagged, I started wondering if I was going to fall between the cracks, attempting two careers at once and failing at both. That would hurt. I was still my father's son. Oh, I might act as if I could float above the usual scramble for worldly gain. But inside I was deeply competitive. I wanted a medal, the big prize, recognition. I fantasized about talking on TV. Isn't that one of the great validators in American society—"As seen on TV"?

But wasn't Christ a loser? One of the greatest losers in history? He didn't just suffer; he lost everything in the end, by all worldly appearances. Was I ready to follow him up that hill? Well, no, actually, I wasn't, even though I realized vaguely that losing could be a kind of freedom. "Huzzahs to those who failed," said Whitman. Losing was a gift. It opened us up to mercies that we couldn't receive otherwise.

Rilke had written that we make spiritual progress by being defeated by increasingly larger things. But the more I focused on my false selves, the healthier they seemed to grow. I wanted to be a success at losing, so I knew that I wasn't succeeding at failing either.

As we approached Lent, I also began to realize that I couldn't even get my story straight.

I had the notion of someday writing a book about What Happened to Me on My Way to Becoming a Catholic. I was taking notes, saving my RCIA handouts, and thinking about narrative arcs. In the back of my mind, I started writing blurbs for the book jacket: "An updated *Pilgrim's Progress*, an amazing story relevant to our modern age."

I found this image in one of my files:

> I see myself and the older man. He has his arm around my shoulders, with one hand steady on the back of my neck. We're standing in front of a jet engine roaring at full throttle. He's gently but very firmly forcing me to kneel down, and he puts my face into the full blast of the engine. But the jet blast is actually a stream of pale fire, with tiny gold flecks and sparkles. I understand: This is a stream of blessings, and I'm trembling now, my knees buckling as he presses me down and talks to me in a quiet voice, like a patient coach or a doctor or a midwife, and he's saying, "You can take it. You can do this," keeping my head down, and I feel the fire peeling away my skin, the blessings shredding my old face off and revealing a new one, then another one under that and then another, though never the one I expected.

Excellent. That described exactly what I was going through right now. I could use it in the book.

There was only one catch. I'd written this four years ago, before any of this Catholic stuff had happened. So what was I thinking then? Maybe I'd had a vague premonition of what I would be going through. Or maybe I'd begun a conversion without knowing it. Or maybe I was simply more aware these days of a process that had been going on for decades.

Whatever the case, it was obvious that my clean narrative arc was out of the question. I was lurching, and the more I lurched, the more I wanted to follow a smooth trajectory that would land me on target at Easter—bingo!—into the church and the loving arms of God. But I wasn't learning anything, certainly not in the right order. Maybe I was learning backward?

If so, I thought, maybe that was actually a plus. When we learn something, we say we "get it." But getting anything, possessing it, simply adds another layer to our false self. To the false self, we are what we own. My path would have to become more and more like that Methodist labyrinth I followed the previous spring. The labyrinth didn't work if you knew how far you had to go. Getting lost was how you got where you needed to go.

11

Purification and Enlightenment

I wake to sleep, and take my waking slow. . . .
I learn by going where I have to go.

—from *The Waking*, Theodore Roethke

Just before Lent I decided to give up coffee, meaning caffeine. I'd stopped drinking. And I'd kicked cigarettes years ago. I could do this, too.

Without coffee, I felt small and scattered, but I slept more soundly, and I also remembered more of my dreams. One night I dreamed that I gave a poetry reading. The poems were in a loose, stream-of-consciousness form that I used to call my tumbling style. The reading seemed to go well, but afterward I was sitting on the curb outside the auditorium, crying. Someone, a woman I think, tried to console me. I jerked away, shaking my head miserably and saying "No, no, no! You don't understand! I wasn't *impressive!*"

Then, in the dream, I saw a page with the line: *Long robes come.*

I knew this meant the robes of God. Then I woke up and lay there in the dark. I understood that the dream was about humility. God comes to us even when—maybe especially when—we aren't being impressive.

It was just before dawn. I got up, made myself a cup of decaf tea, and went out to the backyard swing set. I could smell rain a few miles away in the Hill Country. I sat on a swing, sipping my tea, and listened to the distant thunder. Across the neighborhood, the birds were waking up, singing and calling. Everything seemed fresh and beautiful, and God was all over the backyard. He was in the breeze and the smell of the rain, in the pattern of clouds flying overhead. I felt enormously happy and bewildered, almost crying, and my heart kept hurting more and more, and it wouldn't stop. *O Lord, where are you taking me now?*

Lauren gave me a final reading. She put her hands on me, closed her eyes and said, "You have ecstatic energy, especially in your heart. You have to remain grounded, but this is going to be an important spring for you. You're going to receive something very important. You're going to get it."

Get it? What did that mean? I didn't feel as if I was getting much of anything. And besides, what was I doing listening to a psychic reading to begin with? Both Leviticus and the Catholic Church put the big frown on fortune telling—though Lauren's always been right, so far.

Ash Wednesday

Ash Wednesday is the kickoff for Lent. Catholics, or anyone else for that matter, can go to church and have a cross marked with ashes on their foreheads. The ashes are recycled from the palm fronds turned in after the previous year's Palm Sunday. I was told the ashes were a sign of a lot of things: penance, austerity, Christ's retreat in the desert, a reminder of his final sacrifice and our own mortality.

I thought about myself walking down the street with a big black mark on my forehead. I'd be showing my true Catholic colors for the first time in public. After months of wanting to shout to the world that I was joining the church, I suddenly felt self-conscious. Forget about being crucified upside down in a Roman coliseum. What if somebody teased me? And what about going to work all marked up like that? I had read about anti-Catholic riots in America. Even as late as the 1920s, someone had been lynched in the United States for being a Catholic. The Ku Klux Klan lumped Catholics right in there with African Americans and Jews.

I could get ashes at the end of the day or at noon. If I was willing to go through the entire day with ashes, I could get them in the morning. I decided to go for broke, and I went to 8:00 a.m. Mass at St. Austin's. During the service, two Eucharistic ministers, along with Father Tom, were dispensing ashes. Now keep in mind that Tom is a very big guy, so he has big thumbs. Waiting in line, I tried to sidle over to one of the Eucharistic ministers, a small woman, who was making distinct but wispy crosses on foreheads. Sure enough, when I got to the head of the line and it was my turn, there was Tom smiling at me with his big gray thumb. I felt him make two broad swipes on my forehead, down and across. Branded, big-time. Oh well, I might as well be blatant.

When I got to the office, I sat through a ten o'clock meeting with everyone staring at my forehead. They didn't say anything, and I didn't volunteer any information. After the meeting, however, I met the Boss in the hallway. "What's that?" she asked, pointing.

I told her what it meant and how I would be wearing this sign for the rest of the day. She understood immediately. She had studied many religions, and she told me about Hindu markings on the forehead that represent learning, enlightenment, or social caste. Although she didn't seem to be a part of any faith, she accepted religion as a way of life.

So she was cool about the ashes, but she wasn't about my recent work. She asked me to get my project plans and step into her office. I came back, and she shut the door behind us.

We were in there for an hour. She was not happy with my work. I'd been taking longer lunches, still putting most of my energy into reading and prayer every morning, and I guess it showed. The company was hosting a trade show in April, just after Easter. (Interesting timing. Thanks, God.) I had to both organize and promote the event. We had just hired a new events manager, but there was still a backlog of projects on my desk that needed to be finished. "Nothing happens unless I manage every step of the way!" she told me quietly in an ominous tone.

"Give me a deadline and I'll hit it!" I said. "I always make my deadlines!" I was defensive, although I wondered how far I could ask her indulgence. I promised her once again that I'd do my best, which I would, insofar as I could juggle both business and the RCIA. We left it at that. I went back to my office and stewed.

Could I do all this by myself? Well, no. I'd pray. I didn't know if I could take this tension anymore. I needed help. I also knew that the Boss herself wasn't in very good shape. The past year had been difficult for her and the company. She was trying to find more business, and often worked on sales proposals every night until who knows how late. She was going through an uncertain period with one of our largest clients, and she was in a major dispute with a former employee. She was always tense. Worry lines were deepening across her forehead. She really had no one around to help her. In my mind, I saw her performing one of those strongman feats where the guy is pulling a boxcar with a bit in his teeth. Her freight car was rolling, but the split second she stopped pulling with all her might, it stopped.

It would feel strange to put the Boss in my prayers, a sort of intimacy that was unsettling. But that was the only way out of the tension I felt whenever I was around her. Because my office was next to hers, that was pretty much all day long. There was no place to hide. I would have to pray for her and our relationship, and why not, let's throw in the company as well. So I prayed that our relationship would improve, that I would no longer see her as the enemy but as a hardworking boss trying to do her best. Under that steely persona was someone actually being very patient with me. I prayed that I could work more as a part of the team, that I could advance the company and help it grow.

So that was another thing I could try to give up for Lent: anger with resentment, my favorite dish. Lent was going to be tough.

Six Weeks

Forty-eight days till Easter. On the first Sunday of Lent, we would be making another retreat to the gym, and then we would go through a Rite of Sending. That would be followed by a trip to the largest church in town, San José, where we'd attend a Rite of Election and Continuing Confirmation with other RCIA initiates and their sponsors from all over the diocese.

At our gym retreat, Michael talked about Lent as a period of "purification and enlightenment." The previous period of the RCIA, the Catechumenate, had been information-heavy, with classes about Catholic beliefs and culture. This next period would focus more on interior reflection, a period of "prayer, quiet recollection, openness, and meditation more than study."

Could I manage that? I didn't know, but the fact that I was already slipping back into the caffeine pit wasn't a good sign. I'd tried mint tea, but I felt silly—it was like drinking imitation water. Then I drank decaf tea for a while. That was safe enough. But you know, I really like the taste of coffee, so I bought some instant decaf. It was safe, 99.7 percent caffeine free. But then I started drinking six cups in a row; and was that a slight buzz I felt? Okay, maybe, but it was very slight, so cranking it up a click wouldn't hurt, as long as I could control the dosage, and, of course, I could. I was careful. I started mixing decaf coffee with only a teeny trace of the hard stuff. But the amount of regular instant coffee in my cup began to grow almost magically. I tried adding a bit more decaf to maintain the proportions, but I only wound up with a wicked-strong cup of coffee. Finally one morning I decided to hell with it. I'd quit after Lent. I retrieved my friend Mr. Coffeemaker from the pantry and went back to the usual grind.

At the retreat, Michael told us that you didn't necessarily have to give things up for Lent. You could add something: doing service, for example, or making an extra effort to be nice to someone. (Pray for the Boss.) You could even take a different route to work. The point was to change your life in some way so you could see things with fresh eyes. "Look at what you value," he told us. "What would it mean to give that up?"

Then we broke into small groups and talked about our progress through the RCIA so far. I'd been rehearsing what I was going to say for a week, but as I rattled on, I noticed that I liked the sound of my voice less and less. Everything I said seemed overproduced.

After we joined again into one group, Michael asked us for a favor. We were going to go through a series of rites for the rest of Lent: the Penitential Rite for baptized candidates like me, then a series of three Scrutinies for the catechumens, initiates who hadn't been baptized. As a part of the rites, a series of petitions would be read, asking us to reject our sins. To help him write these petitions, Michael wanted us to write down our sins on pieces of paper and put them in a bowl. The papers would be unsigned, and as soon as he had reviewed them and written up the petitions, he would destroy them.

We all retired to the far corners of the gym to meditate. After ten minutes, I looked over my sin list: pride, anger, self-pity, the sin of talking constantly in my head and not listening to others, the sin of self-involvement. The sin of resenting my family for getting in the way of my work. The sin of not smiling more.

Even a few months ago, using a word like sin would have felt strange, but now I was slinging it around all the time. I had learned that our ideas about sin can be a club to beat ourselves with, but they can also be a diagnostic tool we use to identify and gauge our distance from God. The word, in fact, is way more complicated and subtle than I had thought, like a lot of other things about Christianity.

I looked through my list. Was that enough? You never wanted to be the first in class to hand in your test. But others were putting their papers in the bowl, so I figured it was safe to hand in mine as well.

At 11:30 we assembled for Mass. Once more we initiates all stood with our sponsors in front of the congregation. From the altar the congregation always looked smaller, only a few hundred instead of the thousand or so it sometimes seemed. This was my parish, now. I could recognize dozens of faces in the crowd. As Father P.J. spoke a blessing over us, a 1970s tune from Sister Sledge was going through my head:

We
are
fam-
i-
ly!
I got all my sisters with me!

You bet I got family. God had brought me to this parish, and I felt it was a beautiful fit. It was large enough to escape feeling like a small town, but not so large that I felt lost in the sauce. Some families drove more than twenty miles each way to attend. It was more than a neighborhood parish, but a parish that people deliberately chose as their faith community.

At the altar we wrote our names in a Book of the Elect, pledging our commitment to joining the church. I liked the way Catholics made you sign on the dotted line. At the end of the rite, we stepped down from the altar and recessed down the center aisle, with everyone in church raising their hands over us in benediction. I passed Lauren and the boys and waved, the way I did every Sunday at our dismissal. Harrison and Lauren smiled, and Spencer waggled his hand furiously from the pew.

That afternoon, Lauren and the boys stayed home while I went to San José. This church has served tens of thousands of Catholics, mainly the Hispanic community, since 1939. The church building itself holds over sixteen hundred, and today we were going to fill it up to the balconies.

Our little group from St. Austin met on the outside steps. People were arriving from as far away as Waco, a hundred miles north. I felt as if I was at something between a high school graduation and a political convention. When I was younger, I'd always looked down my nose at ceremonies. I'd skipped my senior year in high school, so I missed out on a high school graduation ceremony. I boycotted my baccalaureate ceremony in college because I was too cool to participate in something so obvious. In fact, the only formal rite of passage I'd ever gone through was my wedding. Now I was making up for those losses with all these rites, and once more I appreciated that the church was a good psychologist. If you want something to stick, you go through it over and over. Through the RCIA, initiates go through four major rites plus dozens of mini-rites and benedictions. Every time I turned around, somebody was showering me with a blessing, and I never got tired of the experience. I was winning the lottery every day.

When everyone in our group had arrived outside the church, we took our places inside. You sometimes hear these days that religions are dying out, that they aren't relevant anymore to our modern times, but you could have fooled me from the size of the crowd that day. During Mass, when we all joined hands and recited the Lord's Prayer, the sound was massive, and I had the happy, reassuring sense of becoming a member of a huge, wonderfully diverse family in the diocese that was a part of an even larger family around the world. There are more than a billion Catholics on the planet right now. I had family.

The one big disappointment was the exorcism. I wasn't expecting Linda Blair exactly, with initiates spinning their heads around and spewing green bile. But I was hoping maybe for something a bit more dramatic than the few words the bishop spoke, something about removing from us all unbelief and hesitation in faith. But that was fine. Catholic culture wasn't the exotic Guatemala it had seemed to me a year ago. Now it was more like Hawaii, where the culture is pleasantly different but it's still a part of the United States and everybody speaks English.

At the end of the rite, we initiates were now among the "elect." We still had to go through the sacraments of initiation, and we still couldn't receive communion. But I was now, technically speaking, a member of the church. If I got run over by a bus tomorrow, I could be buried as a Catholic.

Five Weeks

Forty days to go. The Sunday Mass this week would include the Penitential Rite for candidates, so I would be one of the initiates kneeling in the center aisle while a priest blessed us and we asked forgiveness.

Was I ready for all that? I was thinking about taking my first confession, but I was still looking for the right priest, somebody very old and kind, perhaps with a hearing problem. I thought of my sin list from the retreat. Forget working on the sins themselves for now. I just wanted to do some accounting at this point, get an overview.

Perhaps significantly, this was when I stumbled across a few videos in the church library by Megan McKenna on Christ's parables and social justice. I watched a tape one morning before the family was up, sitting in my jammies and bathrobe, with a notebook. McKenna talked about the parable of the workers who were called at different times of the day to work in the vineyard. The workers who put in a full day felt cheated when they saw that the other workers who put in less time got the same wage.

In the tape, McKenna said, "This parable is all about one question: Who do you *not* want with you in the Kingdom of Heaven?" The question hit hard. I had always had a sense of just deserts. I was that student who worked an extra two hours for those final two points on the test. Then there was the matter of me and my parents. There they were, dancing in heaven perhaps, while I had to stay here and do my homework.

Who would I not want with me? The poor? The marginalized? Social justice had always been one of those issues I had acknowledged and then cheerfully ignored. Should I feed the poor? I'd rather retire to a study and manicure my sensibilities. However, social justice was another example of that Christian bumper sticker, No Divisions. "At the end of the day," said Simone Weil, "we measure our spiritual progress by how we love our neighbor."

With this in my mind, I attended an RCIA class on social outreach. We talked about the marginalized and the poor and how we could help them. Someone from the parish told us about St. Austin's program for helping young homeless kids who lived on the streets around the university neighborhood. It seemed that everyone was saying all the right things about helping the poor, so I threw out the confession that helping poor people was one of the things I really, really didn't want to do. To be honest, I'd rather ignore them. Believe me, I was simply trying to get the class discussion away from the usual clichés, maybe goose it along a little bit. But when I said I'd rather ignore the poor, a nun sitting on the other side of the room suddenly sat up.

My wise-guy act wasn't going down too well with Sister Mary William. I'd never talked to her, but I'd seen her in class because she was a sponsor for one of the initiates. She was seventy-five years old, and I knew that she had worked for many years at the St. Vincent de Paul program at St. Mary's. In other words, working for the poor. I saw her catch herself and then say to me, in a very even tone that I should be ashamed, yes, ashamed of myself. No one should ever, ever, have that attitude.

It was just a single comment. It's not like she lambasted me in front of the class for thirty minutes. I was just trying to liven things up a bit, okay? And besides, if you can't be totally candid in these RCIA classes, where can you be? The RCIA was a kind of sanctuary, and I felt like a mallard shot out of season. No fair! At the same time, I couldn't argue with what she had said. I was acting as if it were okay for me to be honest, as long as others weren't so honest with me.

After class, I tried to say something to her, at least good-bye as I left, but she was talking to someone, and I don't think she heard me. I walked out under a cloud, thinking, *She hates me*.

After class, we went to 11:30 Mass. I joined the other candidates in the center aisle as we knelt down with Father Alan for the Penitential Rite. Conversion, fast or slow, is a burning house with many stories, and I imagined myself in the middle of the flames, unhurt and praying, and the harder I prayed, the more the house burned until the floor broke apart and I dropped down to the story below, then the one underneath. I had burned through so many stories to reach this moment, and now I was reaching the ground, the true bedrock I'd been trying to find for years. As I knelt on the marble, I felt I was kneeling on Christ himself, on his very identity, solid, permanent, and very real.

Father Alan asked the congregation to stand for a blessing over us, and as everyone stood up on both sides and raised their hands over me, I had the sensation of dropping even more. Father went down the line, blessing each of us, and I felt his large, strong hands on the top of my head, very earnest as he pressed down even further and said a blessing.

After Mass, I went home and told Lauren all about it. Spencer was still too young and in his nonstop squirmy phase, so Lauren was staying home with the boys while I was going to Mass. I also told her about me and Sister Mary William's comment.

"Hey, that's great!" she laughed. "You're not a real Catholic till you get chewed out by a mean nun!"

"She didn't chew me out, and she's not mean," I said, offended and a bit alarmed, as if Sister could hear us. "She's really very sweet. She was just being honest."

"Well, I'm glad you had the experience anyway," she said, patting me on the shoulder. "It's an important part of your Catholic education."

Four Weeks

More and more I kept thinking about all the lousy things I'd done in my life. Every time I remembered something new, I saw this little compact mirror jump up like a jack-in-the-box and a scratchy toy voice that said, "Hello-o-o-o-o, jerk-face!"

It was maddening, like a tune I couldn't get out of my head. I was going through the wincing stage, just like my first year in recovery. I also knew from the program that the wincing would soon blossom naturally into cringing. That would be normal, a part of the conversion process.

Being sorry wasn't enough. Megan McKenna talked about the parables as an arrow that cuts us open. She said we have to ask ourselves where the knife blade fits in our lives, where it cuts for us. "What would it take to change your life?" she asked in the tape. "What would it take for you to apply, truly apply the parables to your life today?"

I didn't want to hear that.

On Sunday, out of the blue, Michael asked us, "What's holding you back? What's keeping you from taking that last step?"

I was shocked. Holding me back? Was he out of his mind? For weeks I'd been going as fast as I could. I was an old Model T, a flivver that was roaring down the highway above all prudent speed limits. Everything was shaking, fenders about to fly off, gaskets ready to blow. I wasn't worried that I was going to have a mental breakdown, mind you. I just didn't feel that all my bolts were securely tightened.

I wanted desperately to be an "A" Catholic. It wasn't good enough to get a B, and I certainly didn't want to be a failing Catholic, a remedial Catholic. I felt helpless. I couldn't simply "try harder." In fact, trying seemed to get in the way. And nobody had ever made a deal with Jesus. Nobody had ever worked out a contract with him, saying, "If you heal me, then I'll have faith," or "I'll believe in you, but then you owe me one. You've got to give me salvation." All the lepers, the tax collectors, the centurions, and the bleeding woman had simply said, "Help me. Please. I believe in you." In their pain, they were beyond negotiation. And Jesus told them that their faith had healed them, but that wasn't a deal. It was simply the truth.

I wasn't praying as much as I had in the past. Odd how often the times I needed to pray the most were the times I prayed the least. But early one morning I sat down at the kitchen table and asked Jesus what I should do.

You need to love. You have to learn how to love.

"But I do love you!"

You try. You think you do. But if you did, you would give up your life. You would climb the cross, and you haven't.

"Help me!"

Love me, then. Dying is so easy. It's only your pride that makes it look hard. If you weren't so proud, you wouldn't be so scared.

I brooded for a few days, and then sat down at the kitchen table again, hoping for some consolation.

"Jesus, I'm still scared."

So was I.

"But you're the Son of God!"

I'm also human. Filled with blood, just like you.

I was running out of excuses. "I see you telling me, 'Come to me and die.'"

Only because you have to die to live. That's why I've been calling you so clearly. And you have to do it now. Otherwise, you'll be in misery and torment, and it won't get any better, only worse.

Christ was making me nervous. To be honest, he scared me. I still wanted to join the church, absolutely, but the only way inside was through him, and I saw him more and more as a threat. *Lethal* was the word that kept coming up. I thought of him as a sword, some sort of razor. In fact, I identified with the demons that Christ exorcised in Mark 1:24: "Have you come to destroy us?" The Holy Spirit seemed like one of those caracara hawks I'd seen while driving down to the abbey, watching me as I tried to pass by unnoticed. I kept thinking about the passage in John 3 about Christ being compared to the bronze serpent in Numbers 21, the one that cured the Israelites from poison. Only now, it seemed that Christ himself was the poison. When I closed my eyes, I saw the head of a viper, not striking but waiting, staring a hole straight through me.

I couldn't move forward. Couldn't move back. But Christ was patient (I was told). He would understand (I hoped). So I took this fear to him.

"Jesus, what I'm really scared of is you. You're supposed to be this wonderful figure of love and comfort, but I'm afraid you're something dangerous, a poison, a razor."

You call me what you have to. That, and what you think is dramatic. You have a little theater in your mind, and you're the hero. You're the playwright, the producer, and all the actors. You're the audience. And that will be hell for you: alone with just your thinking, forever.

So I was alone in a room that had sixteen doors, and every door was marked "No Exit" except for one. I wanted to turn every mirror in my house around so I wouldn't have to look at my face, and even that, I knew, wasn't the right way. It was just being melodramatic. It was the pride of self-loathing, the sin of boasting my sin.

Peace is my gift, he said. *Accept my peace.* But I wasn't ready yet. I couldn't open that sixteenth door.

At work, the Boss was losing her temper, not just with me but with everything. The company wasn't in bad shape, but it wasn't moving ahead fast enough. Too many designers were "on the bench," waiting for new assignments. She decided that we needed a corporate retreat, so we congregated at a peaceful resort on Lake Travis for a day of presentations and team-building exercises.

After a morning filled with pie charts and bullet points, we gathered for strategic game playing on the lawn. We split into two teams and were given wooden planks and flags. The object was to find some way to arrange the planks so that one team could reach an "island" of planks in the center of the lawn, retrieve the flag and then get to the "shore," all within an hour. It was harder than it looked. After forty-five minutes I took a break, along with several of the older managers. We'd all gone through this company rah-rah stuff before. Some of the young designers were goofing around with the planks. The Boss was by herself on the island.

I watched her growing more impatient with everyone, trying to get her team organized until she started screaming. "Listen to me! Everybody has got to work together or we're going to die on this island!!"

At least she took the game and what it represented seriously. To the Boss, business was definitely war by other means. But alone on that island is how I remembered her that day: frustrated and out of breath, marooned in the middle of her own company.

Harrison was slowly drifting out of control at school, and Lauren and I were panicked. His teacher, her assistant, and the school counselor had met to talk about his performance. He could do the work, but he kept floating "off task," staring out the window while the other students dutifully plugged away at their exercises. The other students were complaining that he wasn't carrying his own weight. The staff had suggested, putting it delicately, that he might have attention deficit disorder. Both Lauren and I knew ADD kids. Maybe we were in denial and we just couldn't see the similarity. But whatever the problem was, it seemed to be getting worse. It looked as if Harrison was going to get thrown out.

After three hours of discussion, the staff had agreed that they were out of options. Maybe he could go to a special school in the district for children with severe learning problems. Lauren and I talked it over that evening in bed. "Has Harrison said anything to you?" I asked.

"He says he's being a Gandhi."

"What does that mean?"

"Actually, he said a negative Gandhi," she said. "He sees himself doing a kind of nonviolent protest."

"What's he protesting?"

"Maybe the school."

"That's a good school!" I said. "Those are hardworking teachers. They've bent over backward to help him."

"It's not the teachers. Maybe it's the culture. Sure, it's an excellent school, but he's been there for three years, and how many friends does he have? How many playdates did he have last summer with boys in his class? And remember how we all went to the carnival last year and didn't feel like we really fit? Every other boy in his class is only interested in sports and superheroes. Harrison talks about ideas and science. He doesn't want to play soccer. He wants to sit at a computer."

"That sounds like creeping elitism. I mean, is his social life the problem? Just because he has a poster of Einstein in his bedroom—"

"I don't mean that. There are other kids in his class who are just as smart. Maybe smarter, I just think we're a PBS family in a NFL school."

"So what's left?" I asked.

"Private school, maybe. If we can find the right one. If we can get in."

"If we can afford it. Which we can't."

"That's true. We'll just have to pray," she said.

"Ah. Right. I keep forgetting."

While Lauren is a mystic and a healer, she's also extremely organized, especially when it comes to her kids. She started investigating every private school in town.

Meanwhile, I had to spend more time at the office. Our trade show was coming up in a few weeks. We had reserved most of the Austin Convention Center, and now we had to fill it. The show evoked in me all the primal fears we have when we throw a party and then wonder if anyone will show up. I had sent out an e-mail invitation to 30,000 and got 150 replies. We needed at least 600 preregistered attendees to feel safe. It would be a disaster—for me especially—if we couldn't fill the hall. I sent out a direct-mail campaign, as well as a fax campaign. There would be last-minute ads in the newspaper. Slowly, very slowly, the number of preregistrants crept up, but it was like pulling a boxcar with a bit in my teeth.

Then on Monday, we learned that the Boss had been injured. She and her husband had gone to a business conference in Seattle the week before. That weekend they decided to go skiing in Canada. I didn't know the Boss could ski. Maybe she couldn't. On one of the advanced slopes, she took a hard fall, seriously twisting her right knee. They had to carry her off the slopes in a stretcher. She was able to limp onto a plane and fly back to Texas, but the knee was badly torn up. She needed an operation as soon as the swelling went down.

She showed up for a few days after her accident, pulling herself very deliberately down the hall in a full-leg cast. She looked determined, like a wounded king in Shakespeare, moving slowly but still dangerous. She eventually chose to spend most of her time at home while she recovered, managing the company through phone calls and a storm of e-mails.

When I told Lauren about the Boss's accident, she wasn't surprised. "That makes all the sense in the world," she said. "She threw herself off a mountain, and nobody was there to catch her."

Three Weeks

The following Sunday in RCIA, I suddenly found that I couldn't talk. After months of being the first to speak out in every class, after rehearsing my comments during the week and then saying things I never expected to say, after blurting and interjecting and holding forth, I now felt excruciatingly self-conscious. I just clammed up.

Other initiates who had said almost nothing all year were beginning to open up. One woman started talking about paintings of Christ that she'd always loved. A young man, terminally shy, started quoting poetry. This was wonderful to watch. As we moved toward Easter, the whole class seemed to be accelerating rapidly.

But I wanted to delete everything I had said for the past eight months. Michael would ask a question, and the schoolboy inside me was waving frantically. "Me! Call on me!" Instead, I'd bite my lip and tell myself, "Shut up, will you? Just shut up and let somebody else talk!"

I only felt embarrassment for everything I had been saying for months. I had a strong desire to go around to everyone in class, kneeling and thumping my head on the carpet three times in front of them. "Please forgive me, my brothers and sisters, for I have been a Big Mouth."

I moved into heavy cringing mode at this point. Looking at myself in the mirror, I seemed massively self-involved, and that assessment itself seemed self-involved. I wanted to curl up in a little ball. I thought of those TV sets from the fifties—you turn off the set, and the picture jumps back into a little dot in the center of the screen that slowly fades away. I wanted to be like that dot. Just ignore me. I'll be gone in a second.

I knew I wasn't ready for Easter. One evening after dinner, I was taking a walk around the block. I saw myself wrapped in a red cellophane wrapper, stiff and crinkly, like a heavy, plastic snakeskin. I was trying to push it away, shed it somehow. "Please, Jesus, take this away!" Then on the sidewalk in front of me, I saw in my imagination a smooth, round egg, wet, as if just laid, and I knew that inside was an infant who would die without my help.

⚮

That Sunday, Sister Mary William gave a class on something or other, I can't remember what. She was in her seventies, cheerfully disorganized, all over the map. I remember that she said we could say *shit* and not go to hell and that we could wear a medal and chain or not, it didn't make any difference. The rest of her presentation was a blur.

What I do remember, like a diamond point of light, was her spirit and how that spirit filled the room. She had a strong personality, and she spoke her mind clearly, even bluntly at times. But the love she showed us was pure sweetness and one of the greatest gifts I received in the entire RCIA process. Listening to her was like meeting your grandmother for the first time, and she turns out to the best grandmother in the world. At the end of the class, she went around the room, giving everyone a hug. She even hugged me, though I went away wondering if she still thought I was a cold character.

I sent her an e-mail the next day, thanking her. She wrote back and thanked me for thanking her. "Ten were healed," she added in the e-mail, "but only one returned."

On Friday, the Boss went through surgery. Afterward, her husband dropped by the office. He said the operation was a success, but she was in so much pain that she was throwing up. "She says it feels like they cut the leg off," he told us. A dark part of me was pleased. I wanted her to suffer the same way she'd made others unhappy.

So was I ready to join a church based on the love of Christ? Obviously not. But I hadn't confessed any of these dark thoughts to anyone yet, so maybe I could still sneak in under the radar, and nobody would know. Just God, of course.

Two Weeks

The big question was whether I really want to be healed. I didn't answer. I didn't want to open that sixteenth door. Instead, I kept working through the sludge in the bottom of my heart. The more I found what I didn't want to see, the more I found myself thinking about all those lepers healed by Christ. I did a search for *leper* on the Internet.

A library of deformity came up, along with photographs. A lot of photographs. I stared at the monitor. This is what Christ healed, what he pressed with his fingertips, what he embraced.

As I mentioned before, I was born with one hand. This is no tragedy, especially compared with what I saw on the Internet. I could have outgrown being self conscious about my hand, but the self-consciousness was still there, a stubborn lump on my psyche that I kept touching fondly.

I'd read the healing stories as examples of how we should help those in need. We should be like Christ. But now I thought more about the lepers themselves. I realized that it actually took a lot of gumption for them to even approach Christ and ask to be healed. I imagined them as they stared at Christ from a distance, aching and hoping, but knowing they'd be breaking the law if they even entered the town. I saw them as they finally decided *to hell with it* and started walking toward Christ. The villagers turned around, suddenly aware of these hideous, unclean people, and as the lepers approached, I saw the crowd parting in front of them, people staring at them with outrage and disgust. Maybe some of the villagers were angry even at Jesus for attracting these lepers in the first place. And I imagined the lepers thinking, *Yes, I know. I know what I look like. And I know what you're thinking. I'm breaking the law. But I don't care anymore. I've got to ask this man for help.*

We talked in RCIA about Christ healing the lepers. I told Michael what had occurred to me about the courage the lepers had showed when they asked to be healed.

"Yes, they came to Christ with courage," Michael replied. "But also need. More than anything else, they had to admit their need for him."

Now, in the last few days before Holy Week, I remembered that conversation. If I was the leper, if I thought I was deformed and sick in my soul, I'd have to reach out. At Mass, we all join hands to say the Lord's Prayer. It was an uncomfortable moment for me because

I always anticipated the moment when someone turned to take my right hand and—found nothing there. I worried especially about the children, who can be naturally startled by the unexpected. In Mass, for the rest of my life, I would be turning to my neighbor, asking in effect, "Please take my hand." That would be my role and—yes—my blessing.

Accept, accept, the little voice kept saying. *That's all you can do.*

Blessings don't happen in a vacuum. As I went through Lent, I began to understand how my conversion was affecting the people around me. More to the point, I was learning how much it was costing my marriage, my family, and even my job.

Lauren kept trying to talk to me about her own spirituality, but I kept edging away. If it wasn't Christian, I didn't want to hear about it. One evening, we were reading in our bed. It was big and comfortable, the one we inherited after my parents had passed away. On the wall behind us, we had hung a quilt that my grandmother had made years ago, red and white in a pattern called "drunkard's walk."

Lauren mentioned a new book on something, reincarnation I think, and I immediately bristled. I didn't say anything, not a peep, but with Lauren, I have a glass head.

"I can feel what you're thinking!" she said, shutting the book. "Look, I understand why you don't want to talk about this—"

"You're right. I don't."

"—but I'm feeling very, very alone these days!"

"We talk . . ."

"We need to talk more! That's one of the foundations of our marriage! That's one of the ways we make love! And now I can't talk to my best friend about the most important change that I've ever gone through!"

"I think I'm being understanding," I said.

"And I'm being brave!"

"Why?"

"Because I'm scared! Scared for our marriage!"

Now she definitely had my attention. "Okay, let's talk. What are you feeling these days?"

"You're here, but you're not here. Half the time you're off by yourself reading and praying and crying, and that's fine. But it's been a *real* sacrifice for the people who love you the most."

She rolled over to my side of the bed and put her hand gently on my cheek. I knew that gesture. It meant *listen closely: incoming.* "Look, you're having an affair."

Now she really, really had my attention.

"You're having an affair with the Mother Church. Incense, perfume, the way she makes you feel inside." A slight smile. "You've fallen in love with everything about her, completely, absolutely, shamelessly, and why not? She's the church! I understand that, and besides, what could I say? I really think—and the boys feel this, too—that any time you spend with us is taking you away from what you really love right now." She touched my hand. "But if you really take this conversion process seriously, if you really, really want to know the implications of what you're doing, you have to realize that it's been pretty bleak for me and the boys."

"I'll try—I don't know—to be here more, spend more time . . ."

"So far, it's been manageable. We'll all be patient. And you haven't been fired. Yet."

"I do a good job at work! I make my deadlines!"

She sat up. "But your heart isn't in it, and they know that! You get paid to be enthusiastic. You're expected to create excitement about that company, and you haven't, not by a mile. You've been doing the bare minimum." She added, "Just like Harrison at school."

We both took a breath. She'd torn off a big chunk of reality right there, and I knew I'd have to chew on this for quite a while. "Maybe I'll be in better shape to talk later on," I said.

"I hope so, because I've been more upset than you know. I just see us becoming like one of those old freeze-dried couples you see in cafeterias with the Early Bird Special, just sitting there and not saying a word to each other."

"We can't have that."

"No, sweetie. That's what I'm saying. We can't."

Early that week, I went to my first confession. I sat down with a priest at a table, just us alone in a room, and I started to talk. He was the elderly priest I'd been looking for, although there was nothing wrong with his hearing. I told him the worst things I'd ever done, tearing them out "like rotten teeth," as Merton said in his autobiography. The priest didn't flinch. I'm sure he'd heard everything over the years, from all sorts of people. As I continued, he seemed very sad at times. In the end I confessed that I couldn't accept fully the fact that God loved me. That seemed to disturb him the most. I was surprised and, when I thought about it, impressed that he was most concerned about that. As penance, he gave me readings from the Bible to study, all of them talking about how God loves us. "Remember how much you're loved," he said as I left, and I hoped that one day I'd fully agree.

I wanted the Rite of Reconciliation on Thursday to be more of the same as my confession. As it turned out, the rite itself didn't speak to me. I can't remember the homily. There were six priests for confession, no waiting, but the one I chose didn't seem to be very engaged. It was all very quick and perfunctory and over in a few seconds. That showed me that there wasn't anything magical and automatic about the rite if I wasn't engaged myself.

But something else happened that evening. When I had arrived, the church was still half empty. For some reason, I moved over one space from the aisle when I took my seat. As we all stood up at the beginning of the service, I felt someone move into the space next to me.

It was Sister Mary William! She winked at me. I winked back and gave her a nudge with my elbow, like we'd been buddies for all this time. All during the service, we chatted quietly. She told me about her social services at St. Mary's, working for St. Vincent de Paul. We talked about anger, about twelve-step programs, about the Holy Spirit. I sat there, quietly amazed. Afterward she gave me a big, big hug. I felt like I was sprinkled with fairy dust, cleansed and blessed to the bone.

The Saturday before Palm Sunday and Holy Week I drove up into the expensive hills west of Austin to bring the Boss some soup.

It was my wife's idea. I felt out of place in all that prime real estate. The Boss and her husband had a split-level, majestic barn of a house set into the hillside. It was very impressive, with magnificent views. When her husband let me in, I saw that the rooms were half empty, as if they both were just passing through. He said that the Boss was staying in one of the first-floor rooms, since she could barely negotiate the stairs.

When I walked in, she was lying on a mattress in a bare room with papers scattered around her and a laptop in front of her. She seemed surprised to see me. She looked like a little girl, home from school with a bad cold. Hardly the Captain Ahab I had in mind. We chatted a bit, I gave her the soup, and then I fled.

When I got home, Lauren said that the Boss had called. Oh, brother. But she had called to thank us for the soup. "Actually," said Lauren, "she told me that nobody had ever given her anything like that before, and I swear, her voice was shaking a little bit."

That gave me pause. And I kept on pausing. This was the person I hoped was suffering. I was sorry now for that hope, but being sorry wasn't good enough. As McKenna had put it, "What would it take to change your life?"

12

Joining the Family

Easter came late that year. We were already moving into the last of spring. The days were getting warmer, almost summery. Grass covered the hillsides along the freeways, and the bluebonnets and fire wheels were in full bloom. I was excited and anxious, but somehow at peace. Maybe God was indeed pouring peace into my heart. Or maybe I had just tizzied myself to a standstill. Maybe it was both. During Holy Week I began to feel a colossal sense of *Let It Be*.

Still, Lent seemed to take forever. But I gradually figured out that the season isn't about holding your breath but rather finding a new way to breathe. In fact, it would always be Lent. I would always be just a few days away from being a "real" Catholic.

I asked the Boss for Friday off, telling her about Easter week, and she wrote back by e-mail, "Yes, of course. I know how much this means to you. May it be everything you envision."

The whole week was like that. There were rude bumps along the way, but it was a period of growing calm and reconciliation, like my experiences with Sister Mary William and the Boss, puzzle pieces coming together with unexpected gifts and understandings.

Michael met with each of us individually and asked if we were ready to take the final step. I told him about a saying in my recovery program, that the program ruins your drinking. It's a joke, of course, but it refers to a serious change in people who stay with the program. After a point, after listening to hundreds and thousands of stories about drinking, you simply know too much to accept self-destruction as a viable career. You can ignore what you've learned, of course. You can always falter. But it gets harder the more you know. In the same way, even though I knew such a tiny bit about being a Catholic Christian, I still felt that I knew too much to go back.

Was I ready to join the church? I couldn't say. As an initiate, was I "doing it right"? Beats me. If my conversion was a movie, it was still just a rough edit, with jump cuts, repetitions, and spaghetti narratives that kept looping back on themselves. But when Michael asked me if I wanted to join the church, I said yes. Absolutely and positively yes. I didn't have a nanosecond of doubt. Ready to join and wanting to join were two different things. I was just grateful that the invitation was still open, and I felt—no, I knew for sure—that if I didn't step through the open doors of the church, I would be turning my back on the greatest opportunity of my life.

I still couldn't close my eyes and "see" Christ. My personal Christ was a kind of hole in the doughnut. Here I was, entering a Christian church, and I couldn't say for sure whether I actually had a relationship with Jesus. In fact, I was still scared of him. I couldn't shake the sense that Christ was something lethal. Lauren had given me a Catholic medal of the Holy Spirit the week before. I loved wearing it, but when I leaned forward, I could feel the chain flip across the back of my neck, and it made me think of a snake turning: Christ as a viper. But no, I told myself, that wasn't it. He wasn't venom. He *took* the venom. He drank that cup for all of us. That's what Holy Week is about. He was with me, I told myself, even if I couldn't see him.

What I could see, or thought I could see, was God everywhere. I used to think that faith was like being in a room and assuming that God was in the next room. You just had to blindly assume he was there. But now I felt that faith was how I *saw* the room, how I was in the room itself. Faith wasn't assuming that something was "there" that wasn't visible. It was more like the laws of perspective. It wasn't what we see so much as how we see.

Everywhere I looked, there were little Post-it notes that said "God." The weather was God. The wind, the rivers, the arrangement of weeds along the freeway was God. God engineers the rain. He maneuvers every drop of water from thousands of feet up in the sky and succeeds in having it land precisely where it does, on target, billions of times a day, all over the world. God's work is everywhere, and if he's in the details, I decided it was because he loves them. His universe could have been an infinite lump. But the Himalayas and a baby's eyelash are equally specific and equally, precisely themselves down to the last atom. Every human deformity, every harelip is crafted with exquisite care. I was even questioning the idea of deformity itself, because the entire universe is so successful in being exactly the shape it is.

And yes, the details include tragedies. This is the God of disasters. The God of anthrax. The God who gives us stillborn babies. I couldn't explain why bad things happen to good people. But I also realized that much of what we take for granted is also God's work. It occurred to me that between each and every heartbeat in every person on the planet, he stops to think and decide whether to keep our hearts beating. He had repeatedly given me the green light for half a century, and for most of that time I hadn't given him a thought. Even the continued existence of the universe is a miracle. There's no reason why it should keep on keeping on. God could flip the switch anytime he wanted, right? And he hasn't. Yet.

For the past year I had sometimes seen myself as a sailing ship on a polar expedition, locked in ice. I was contained by the strength of God. He could crush me like an egg at any second. But now I felt more like a baby chick in his hands. His strength held me up. Those polar images seemed distant now. Ice was melting.

Holy Week

As we entered Holy Week, I looked around the RCIA group during class that morning, and I thought of a rabbinical saying that over every blade of grass in the world, an angel is hovering, saying "Grow! Grow!" So perhaps over each one of us was an angel saying "You're almost there! You can do it!" Who was I not to assume that heaven was indeed filled with cheering angels, for us and everyone else all over the world, on every path that led to God?

Palm Sunday

Christ's entrance into Jerusalem. For a long time, I'd been thinking about why he took that last trip to Jerusalem. He could have stayed away—it would have been more reasonable. He could have remained a teacher. He could have taught somewhere in a nice liberal-arts college. The Crucifixion didn't make sense.

When I had asked Michael why Christ decided to go to Jerusalem, he said that it wasn't a decision. Christ had to go, the way a parent would rush without thinking into heavy traffic to save a child. He also reminded me that if Christ had a choice, it was whether or not the purity of his message could be saved without this final sacrifice.

Maybe it was like Gandhi and Martin Luther King. Gandhi could have been a successful trial lawyer. King could have lived a comfortable life as a pastor in Alabama. But as they understood more clearly the insufferable gap between what was and what should be, they had to move beyond prudence. At a certain point, they had to make a choice about that gap, then bridge it with their own bodies. As Michael said, it wasn't really a choice. They understood too much.

Monday

Like Peter, I was "walking on the waters" of my belief. And like Peter, I was bobbing and sinking and had to be repeatedly hauled up, dripping like a flounder.

At work, I was in the middle of pulling the trade show together, getting tense, walking around with black coffee, hovering over my webmaster and events manager. We needed to make final changes to the website. We needed to send out another mass faxing. I was overseeing the production of the direct-mail postcards, plus the event programs. We needed signs for the hallways, directing people to their classes. Time was running out.

Harrison was still having problems at school. He'd been sent to the principal's office for fighting. He said he was just being "lively." His teacher said he'd "gone berserk." Lauren and I had run out of anything to say, but she was still researching private schools. She had found a Montessori school downtown, and she had an appointment tomorrow to visit the fourth-grade class.

Six days to go until Easter.

Tuesday

Lauren reported back from her trip to Parkside, the Montessori school. It was wonderful. The whole atmosphere was different. Classes were in a hacienda-style building overlooking a courtyard and play areas surrounded by bougainvillea. The fourth-grade classroom, where Harrison would go, was on the second story, with large windows overlooking the trees, so you had the sense of being in a tree house. An aviary was next door, with finches and lovebirds. Everything was green, cool, and quiet. Lauren said that the children were busy, but there was nothing frantic or stressed about the class. Groups of children were working on projects, talking quietly. The class had three computers. A real-live rocket scientist from NASA visited every week. They put on a play every Friday. Their Iowa test scores were often in the 98th percentile. Lauren said all the children seem bright, happy, and sensitive to others.

The school seemed just right for Harrison. Small and filled not so much with competitiveness as with intelligence and sharing. In fact, both Lauren and I would have given our eyeteeth to have gone to a school like that when we were kids. We just had a few small questions, like, where in the world would we find the money to pay the tuition?

At five the next morning, Lauren and I were both awake, whispering to each other over Spencer, who was asleep between us. Lauren said that she'd been awake for an hour, worrying about Harrison, whether he would be a disruption at a new school as well. But she also thought that at Parkside he might bloom. "His eyes might sparkle again."

When Harrison was three or four, he was incandescent. I remember how he would run down the sidewalks in Brooklyn, a little boy with bright blond hair, looking at everything with amazing intensity. People would stop and turn. He seemed to literally shine, and we hadn't seen that light since we came to Texas. For the past three years, he had always been the new kid in class as we moved around to different neighborhoods, changing his schools in an effort to find the right fit for him. So maybe Parkside was the answer.

"That's a lot of money," I said.

"Yes," she said, "but maybe God is blessing us. We've been so focused on whether Harrison is on-task all the time. Is that the point? Maybe our boy is helping us see that there are better ways to live."

Maybe, maybe. I got up and fixed breakfast, thinking about the cost of tuition.

Wednesday

I finished the last details at work. The conference website was up, the faxes sent, the postcards mailed. We now had reached our minimal goal of preregistered attendees for the trade show. Now I could take off without worrying. Thank you, God.

Three days to go. I kept waiting for something dramatic. Lauren had told me that I was going to "get it," but I couldn't see anything to get. I had fantasies about some sort of eleventh-hour crisis, maybe as we entered the church for the Easter Vigil services. It would be like those scenes in old war movies where the platoon is under heavy fire and one of the green recruits gets hysterical. The old sergeant has to slap him around. "Thanks," the recruit says, voice trembling. "I needed that." I saw myself and Michael standing in the wings beside the altar. I was telling him that I just couldn't take that last step. I wanted drama. I wanted a sound track to my life, some sort of crescendo, a cymbal crash as I stepped over the threshold of the church and into the arms of God.

Nothing like that was happening. The days were calm. Birds twittered in the trees. Outside my private head, everything was rolling along as planned. I was vaguely disappointed.

Holy Thursday

I went to services that night at St. Austin's. I remember the Holy Thursday service last year at the Episcopal church. They had stripped the altar, then taken everything else as well. I mean everything: every bowl and cloth, every object for the sacrament, everything that wasn't nailed down. When they were finished, the church reminded me of an apartment the day you move out. What was normally a warm, cozy church now had a barren, cold, depressing look. We had all said a final prayer, turned out the lights, and left in silence.

St. Austin's was bare, but it wasn't shockingly bare. The Episcopalians had done it better. Two young women sat beside me, college students, and they whispered and chattered all through the service. Part of services on Holy Thursday involves the priest and others washing the feet of parishioners, just as Christ had done at the Last Supper. I couldn't see the foot washing from where I sat. The service wasn't working for me. But I thought I could find a value in that. We're moving into a great darkness. I don't need a rich and profoundly satisfying Mass. Maybe it was entirely appropriate that I felt a kind of faltering, a poverty.

At the end of Mass, it was time to remove the consecrated Host from the church. Father Tom got ready to carry it. He had his regular robes: a simple white gown called an alb, with a larger, elaborately embroidered robe over it called a chasuble. The altar servers added an even larger, heavier robe called a cope. Now he looked ready for a hurricane. The ciborium, a cup holding the Host, was taken down from the altar area and given to Tom. He looked even more massive than usual under all those robes, his head down, moving slowly, like a Kodiak bear. He processed down the center aisle as the rest of us were singing in Latin the Pange Lingua: "Sing, my tongue, of the mystery of his glorious body . . ."

Tom and the altar servers made their way down the aisle, and we all followed them out to the street and then into the courtyard and into Hecker Hall, where the ciborium was placed on a table. We gathered around, sang a bit more, and prayers were said by Tom and P.J. and Alan, who had joined them. I looked around the room. There were maybe a hundred of us, and the people in the front were all kneeling. I was struck by how unself-consciously they knelt, right there in front of everyone, and I felt proud to be joining a church and religious culture where public devotion was accepted as a matter of course. I knelt too, feeling the hard floor. When I opened my eyes later on, almost everyone had left. I got up, puffing a bit and rubbing my knees. Three days to go.

Friday

That morning we got a package from Lauren's dad; it was an icon of Our Lady. Lauren remembered it as the only thing her father had inherited from his mother. It was also the only thing he had ever given one of his children from his own family.

"So maybe he didn't exactly hate the church," I said.

Lauren turned the icon around, holding it carefully, and placed it on the mantelpiece. "He hated going to church. But not the church itself."

"So maybe he wasn't the ogre you talk about."

"I'm not making anything up," she said. "When we were kids, it was a Gothic horror show, believe me. It was like *The Shining*, Jack Nicholson chopping through the door. But I think Dad was just scared. He was angry only after we left Seattle, when he had to work in corporate America."

"Like my dad leaving Krum," I said. "He had to leave for the career he thought he needed."

"Right. My dad was a different man in Seattle." She sat next to me on the sofa. "I've told you he loved boats. Once in Chicago, he bought a sailboat, but he couldn't get it to work. It was a disaster. He almost knocked himself out when the boom swung over and hit him. Eventually he sold it, but in Seattle he had a little boat that he built himself. I remember going with him down to this village beside the Sound. He had a shed where he spent Saturday afternoons working on the boat. I'd play around the pier. Those were nice days, very peaceful. He rarely got mad back then. Later, he was really just an anxious suburban dad, trying to do his best."

So Lauren's dad was yet another example of how people could be misjudged. Did we have a theme here? First the Boss, now my father-in-law? And there was one more example.

That week, I heard about Leo, the vice president I reported to in my previous company. He was, in fact, the reason I'd left. I hated him probably more than anyone else I've ever met in business. Up front, let me say that I'm totally not objective about this guy. Before Leo, I was running marketing communications for the company, building the website, producing brochures, and happy to be in my own sandbox. Leo brought in a new manager and placed me under this guy who was competent but, well, he wasn't me. Looking back, I see that I could have lost my job altogether. At least I still had a position. But I lost my office, lost my title, and wound up sharing a cubicle. I was hugely offended—no, I was outraged. I wanted to tear his face off. I said nothing and hunkered down in my cubicle, smoldering. I felt that Leo was the worst thing that had ever happened to the company. What used to be a smart, scrappy little high-energy start-up became instantly stodgy, a middle-aged corporation laboring under Leo's thumb.

Then there was Leo himself. He was a big guy, and he scared me. His very bulk seemed physically threatening. At the same time, and in the same way, he was a mountain of condescension. I can still see that patronizing smirk on his face when someone made a suggestion in a meeting. It felt as if he were patting us on the head like we were little puppies, even though some of us had been in business for decades. (It's odd that when we're complaining about our bosses, it often sounds like we're all complaining about the same person.)

Anyway, I feared him, loathed him, and despised him. I kept waiting for the CEO to wise up and get rid of this idiot, but that didn't happen. Eventually I left the company (and started working for the Boss. Yeah, I know. Brilliant career move).

In the middle of Holy Week, I learned that Leo had been fired. The company still wasn't profitable, and a new investor had demanded a review of the management team. Leo was the only executive who didn't make the cut. Even sweeter, he'd been escorted out the building by security, the same way he'd ordered so many others to be taken out.

I was almost giddy when I heard the news. I hoped he would rot forever in business hell. But the giddiness faded, and I wondered why I had hated him so much in the first place. Was it just a matter of injured pride? That, plus the fact that we were too much alike? I wanted to control my business life as much as he did. I was, in my ingrown, introverted way, as condescending as he was. I was my own Leo.

In conversion, a new person steps out of the rubble of old personality. That's the idea, anyway. I should have left behind my feelings about Leo and bosses and control. Perhaps God was tapping me on the shoulder, offering me a few last learning opportunities concerning me and my stiff neck.

On the way to work, I read a bumper sticker: "My Real Boss Is a Jewish Carpenter." Until I accepted who I really worked for, it wouldn't make sense to join His company.

Friday Night

On Good Friday, I learned that not a single Mass is celebrated anywhere in the world. The entire church is quiet in a special way, with only communion services. Lauren stayed home with the boys while I went to St. Austin's. I walked in and greeted a few parishioners I knew with what I thought was appropriate cheer. They smiled politely and withdrew to their seats. Did I say something wrong? Then I noticed that people were wearing a lot of black. One man was wearing a black tie.

It took a moment for me to get it: This is a funeral. We've had a death in the family. Of course people aren't being particularly chipper. This is an evening of grief.

We went through the quiet service, very simple and stark. We listened to a long, complete reading of the Passion. Acting the role of the crowd, we called "Crucify him! Crucify Him!" After the readings, the priests, P.J. and Tom, went to the back of the church and brought in a large cross. Real large, over six feet tall. Tom shouldered it, and P.J. helped. They slowly processed to the altar and set it down in a footing. Then we all approached in two lines, as if we were taking communion, and kissed the rough wood of the cross.

I've heard the Mass sometimes described as "great theater" in a way that made it seem merely theatrical—not real, somehow. Just playacting. But that night, I could see that, sure, it was theater, but theater as the most involved way we can understand the meaning of the Passion. We were all participants, with priests and parishioners playing our roles. Afterward, I walked back to the parking lot with others, and I could see some with a hunched, please-don't-talk-to-me posture. They were still in the role, and would be until Sunday.

Years ago I had criticized Christianity for not honestly addressing the dark side of life. Hinduism, I said, had gods of both darkness and light. Christianity had a big problem because they insisted on God being completely good. Well, here was the darkness. How far we accept it is up to us. We've been given our role to play.

Saturday Morning: Dawn

I woke up at four. I lay there in the dark, completely awake, like a kid on Christmas morning. In sixteen hours I'd be a Catholic. In sixteen hours I would be receiving full communion. Receiving the body of Christ. Yes, I'd been led by a light that was gradual, but I'd been dazzled every step of the way, and now that light seemed even brighter.

I got up, made some coffee, and walked around the veranda in the early light. Fifteen hours and thirty minutes to go.

I thought about when our boys were born. With Harrison, the birth was extremely difficult: eighteen hours of labor with three hours of pushing. (Guys, that's a lot.) We entered St. Vincent's Hospital in Manhattan at midnight. The next afternoon at four, Lauren was still at it, still pushing through wall after wall of pain. I had brought along a copy of Walt Whitman to the hospital. I don't know where my mind was, but I had the idea that I would read her *Leaves of Grass* while she lay on her back and went through absolute agony. We had a midwife, and midwives can't provide any drug stronger than aspirin. It was natural childbirth all the way, and naturally I never opened the book.

I remember standing beside her hospital bed as she gripped my hand, and I looked out the window at the sun setting over New Jersey and thought, *This ain't going to happen*. At 4:40, the midwife sent me down the hall to get a doctor for a C-section. Then one of her nurses called me back. Harrison was finally arriving, glistening and dark purple from the labor, looking like a little African idol. One last push and he was out. His eyes darted all around as he lay on the examination table. Even just a few seconds old, he had, it seemed, an almost frantic curiosity about the world.

I know some couples (fathers more than mothers) who talk about childbirth as a wonderful gush of emotions. There's pain, yes, but also huge happiness, a great catharsis, tears of joy. When our friends heard about the birth, a lot of them (the ones without kids), all said the same thing: "Oh, you two must have been so happy!"

We wanted to tell them, "Happy isn't quite the word. Stunned? How about stunned?" After the labor, Lauren and I just blinked at each other. It felt as if a two-day hurricane had just passed over us. All we knew was that she was alive, Harrison was alive, and I was alive. Nothing else mattered. There were no tears of joy, no huzzahs. Just a quiet, crystalline point of gratitude. Maybe we were too tired for anything else.

Lauren spent the night in the hospital. The next morning, I walked back to the hospital through an autumn drizzle. I gave her flowers, plus a medal I had found in one of the antique shops in the West Village. It was heart-shaped, with a lavender ribbon. When I visited Lauren and (I was still amazed at the idea) this new child of ours, I pinned the medal to her hospital gown and told her that I'd never seen anyone go through that much pain before. She thanked me in a tired whisper. Her face was puffy, and she had two black eyes from pushing so hard. She looked like a boxer.

Spencer was born in a bathtub in Texas, at a midwife's clinic. With him, labor was much easier, insofar as any labor is easy. After the birth, while Lauren caught her breath, I took him out to the clinic's lobby and sat down. He lay in my arms so calmly, and I thought, *How very, very neat to have this child.* Don't get me wrong. I was absolutely focused on the event. Did I love this baby? Yes, absolutely, from the moment he was born. But my heart wasn't bursting. I was just very happy in a very quiet way.

Now five years later, on Holy Saturday, I walked around the veranda thinking about what was going to happen that day. I reminded myself that whatever I was going to feel would probably be about right. Right for me, at least. Growing up, I often worried that I wasn't having the appropriate feelings. In my family's culture, there's an emotional orthodoxy that we are expected to follow, but I had learned over the years that some of us are less orthodox than others. If I didn't go through this with all the right reactions, so be it. I still didn't get it. I couldn't close my eyes and see Jesus. But I could still slip in under the radar.

Saturday Morning: Retreat

We gathered again in the gym. We're almost there! I felt like I did the morning I got married. I looked at my watch. In thirteen hours, we'd be inside the church, at the altar, and receiving full, I mean *full,* communion. It was hard to explain, but I was completely obsessed with that little wafer and the fact that it becomes the actual body of Christ. It was one of the most wonderful things I could imagine. I was amazed. The gym was filled with light.

Michael led us through the liturgy, telling us where we would stand and what we would say. We broke into groups, little mini-retreats to the distant four corners of the gym, where we talked about any last concerns we might have. Nobody in my group had any worries. The feeling in the room was like a quiet avalanche that was picking up speed. Everyone seemed pumped and ready.

We reassembled after a while, and Michael gave one last talk about communion, how this is a meal that's at the very center of being Catholic, how we are marked by it as "the people of the meal." As he talked, I couldn't stop thinking about the Host. It was like when my parents died. I spent months thinking about each one. It wasn't pain so much as churning, just thinking about them hour after hour, for months. I was thinking about the Host the same way now, only somehow in reverse. It was a process of letting the idea sink in, of accepting rather than letting go.

Michael finished. I snapped back to attention. We were standing up now to form a big circle. With initiates, sponsors, Michael, and the RCIA team, there were more than fifty people, and we filled the gym. We all joined hands. Michael reminded us of the profession we'll be making this evening, and then he said, "Look all around you. Look at the people in this circle. This is the church."

A lightbulb turned on. Here was Christ. I didn't have to close my eyes. He was standing right here, had been standing here all along, invisible and apparent. I looked at the faces smiling at me across the circle. Here he was—with Anna, Tim, John, and Barbara. He was here with Ted and Michael, and Sister Mary William. And the circle included Lauren and my boys. It included all the people who had helped me get to this point by teaching me, or loving me, or just putting up with me and giving me a model of faith and spiritual love. My Baptist friends were here, Steve and Amy, and Cheryl and Bruce. Our Quaker friends, the Inskeeps. Ernie, my t'ai chi teacher who changed my life. Eddie, my mentor in the recovery program. Frank, my friend who was always so patient with me as I held forth about the universe. Martin, my Presbyterian neighbor. Jack, my friend of thirty years. My sister, and Mother and Dad were here, too. And my grandparents and great-grandparents, and all the angels and saints in heaven.

They were all here in the circle, all with Christ, as the body of Christ, and it hurt to look around the circle—I was squinting—because the light seemed so bright in the gym, and all their faces were shining.

Michael said a final prayer. It was time to go, rest up, and return to church that evening. Then he did something that I don't think he'd done all year. He gave us his warmest smile and said, "God bless you."

The blessing settled over us. *This is a man with daughters*, I thought. I loved my boys with all my heart, but I had sometimes seen a special tenderness between dads and their daughters, and that was what I felt as the blessing went through me.

⚬✖⚬

I was still trying to pull myself together as we gathered the metal chairs and stacked them in corners. As I had learned, so much of the modern spiritual life involves the repeated unfolding and folding of metal chairs.

Sister Mary William came up to me, beaming. We hugged, and she pressed something wrapped in tissue paper into my hand. "Listen to what I'm going to tell you," she said. "Native tribes were very careful to carry the fire when they moved to a new camp. So they put some coals in a wrapping and carried it very carefully so a new fire could be started from the old one, so the old fire wouldn't be lost. The person responsible for the safety of the coals was called the fire carrier. I'm giving you something so you can be a fire carrier."

I didn't know what the tissue carried, but my hand was shaking. I swallowed hard, trying not to cry. I wanted to make sure that I understood what she was doing. I asked, "Why am I carrying the fire?"

"For God, for what he wants."

"But who am I carrying it for?"

"For your tribe," she said and added with a smile, "I've been given many, many tribes in my lifetime."

I was in a daze. I was having trouble talking, but I managed to thank her, and we hugged again, and she left.

Outside in the parking lot, I unwrapped the tissue. Inside was a crucifix on a chain. For all I know, she gave one of these to everyone, but that wasn't the point. This was something more than special. I thought of the Holy Spirit medal that I was wearing, and I pulled it out to make sure I remembered what it said: "Fill the Hearts of Thy Faithful and Kindle in Them the Fire of Thy Love."

Fire carrier. And my name is Cole. Lauren had been right after all. I got it. It just wasn't quite what I'd expected.

I drove home, barely, and floated through the house, said hi to Lauren, told her what had happened with Sister, and retreated to the veranda to collapse in a chair and sob until I was out of breath.

I don't want to sound as if I were falling apart, though, of course, I was. All through Lent I had been thinking of the phrase *emotionally incontinent*, and I remembered my dad after his stroke, how much he cried. At this point, however, I wasn't concerned with what I looked like. Everything was imploding. It was just too much. Sister couldn't care less how much I knew or what I did. She simply accepted me, every ounce of me. Her gift, God's gift, was totally unexpected, and that's part of what knocked me out. But more than that, I felt that I'd been given something personalized, marked with my initials. I had the feeling we have with love, when someone recognizes us for who we really are and calls us by our true name.

And even so, this gift wasn't just for me. How would I carry it forward? I didn't know. At the very least I would try to remember. I would try to share this wonderful news.

Easter Vigil

Three hours to go.

I put on my old Brooks Brothers suit from New York, the one I wore to my wedding seventeen years earlier. I also put on the same tie I wore that day. As Lauren got dressed, I hesitated, then put on the crucifix that Sister had given me. I tucked it under my shirt, but Lauren said, "Wear it on the outside, over your tie. If there's one night in your life when you want to be really flagrant about your faith, it's tonight, so show it to the world." So I did. At least for the evening, I'd be *in religio flagrante*.

Before we left, Lauren paused. "I'm very happy to witness all this, to watch you go through it. So thank you."

I remembered the patience she'd shown me over the past two years, keeping her thoughts to herself as I flipped from uncertainty one day to righteous indignation the next, prickly and self-absorbed, and all I could do now was tell her "Thank you, too" and kiss her back.

I still worried that she wasn't a True Blue Catholic, but I remembered what I had heard a few mornings ago when I asked Jesus to help me. I'd been thinking—okay, fretting and stewing—about a spirituality group that Lauren had recently started with some other women. They burned smudge sticks and used rituals from Native American cultures. I told myself that they were just doing what I was doing, trying to find out what worked for them, but I didn't know for sure what was going on. Almost none of the women were connected with any religion at all, and most of them had major issues with Christianity.

So at the kitchen table I asked, "What about Lauren's group?" And then, immediately and quite clearly, I heard the words *My light is everywhere.*

⌀

The sitter arrived for the boys. We wrote out phone numbers, checked the pizza in the oven, and left for the church.

When we arrived, Lauren went out front to find my sister, who was going to attend. I went to the room where we'd met for RCIA classes over the past nine months. Everyone was all dressed up and nervous. I felt as if I were at a prom, or more like a wedding, which, of course, I was.

Ted asked how I was doing. I told him, no last-minute spiritual crises yet. I'd been thinking about whether to carry anything into the church with me. When I lived in New York, I used to go to the Russian steam baths in the East Village. When you checked in at the door, you emptied your pockets. They gave you a locker key, which you wore on a string around your neck. It was ritualistic, having to give up your money, your keys, and all your proofs of identity before you could enter this special area where you would take off your clothes and be steamed and cleaned.

That's what I felt like now. On impulse, I gave Ted everything in my pockets: my wallet with cash and driver's license; the keys to my office, home, and car; a little package knife that I carry; and my watch. Now I had nothing except my glasses, my wedding ring, and my crucifix.

A half hour before Mass, we left the hall and gathered on the sidewalk in front of the main doors to the church. Because St. Austin's is next door to the University of Texas, it faces a busy street, especially on a Saturday night. The sky was almost completely dark, and a wild, gusty wind was blowing from the south. I felt exposed. The servers brought out a Weber kettle, the kind you use for backyard barbecues (you were expecting maybe a stone altar?) and filled it up with wooden sticks. There was a hint of lighter fluid in the air. Lauren was standing at the edge of the crowd. Beside her I spotted my sister, all five feet, three and a half inches of her, peering over the shoulders of the people in front of her. The initiates assembled in front in two straight lines.

At 8:30 they fired up the Weber. I was expecting some kind of sacramental torch, but they used a propane fireplace lighter. Father Alan and the altar servers came out. As Alan went through the ritual, the wind started rising even more. Sparks flew up and swirled over the crowd. We huddled together. A car filled with students passed by, honking, and somebody stuck their head out and yelled something. Alan finished the prayers and then turned to an altar server who was holding the Easter candle, a big one, six feet tall and thick as a two-year sapling. Alan—standing head and shoulders above the crowd, his bald head shining—helped the server catch a flame from the fire with one of the sticks, then held it to the wick of the candle. For a long moment, it looked hopeless, the wind still gusting, ripping the little flame around, but finally, with Father cupping his hand around the wick, it caught and started burning. This was the candle we would use for Easter Day, throughout the Easter season, and for the rest of the liturgical year.

The doors opened. This was it: we were crossing the threshold. I looked up ahead. The inside of the church was black. I mean totally black, black as the bottom of a coal mine at midnight on a moonless night, and I was entering that blackness with nothing but Ted's hand on my shoulder.

We stepped inside, and everything moved into dreamtime. Singing, we slowly processed down the aisle, surrounded by the dark. I was thinking of what the Koran says about Judgment Day, when the only sound will be the shuffle of millions of feet that are marching, marching, marching, and the eyes of the damned are "blue with terror."

We marched along, singing. Ted's hand was still on my right shoulder. I hesitated, then squeezed his hand. He squeezed my shoulder in response. We approached the altar and turned into the front pews reserved for us. The rest of the congregation took their seats, and we began what would be a two-and-a-half-hour Mass. The church was still dark.

The readings began with the beginning, from Genesis, chapter 1, verse 1. A young man was reading the first verses, trying as best he could to give a "dramatic" lift to the words. He reminded me of myself at that age, struggling to be impressive. Myself about three minutes ago, actually. There were many other readings, from Exodus about the parting of the Red Sea, from Isaiah and Ezekiel. Gradually, as we moved through the readings, the lights rose and finally filled the church. The timing for the lights wasn't quite right, but you got the idea.

The Mass didn't feel like two and a half hours, more like a regular Mass, but somehow larger, deeper, and with parts that felt very old and hypnotic. We reached the Litany of the Saints. The cantor sang out the saint's name, and we responded with "Pray for us." It kept going on and on and on and on and on. I was dazzled. I followed the names in the program of the Mass:

> Holy Mary, Mother of God, pray for us
> St. Michael, pray for us
> Holy Angels of God, pray for us

Saint John the Baptist, pray for us
Saint Joseph, pray for us
Saint Peter and Saint Paul, pray for us
Saint Andrew, pray for us
Saint John, pray for us
Saint Mary Magdalene, pray for us
Saint Stephen, pray for us
Saint Ignatius, pray for us
Saint Lawrence, pray for us
Saint Perpetua and Saint Felicity [two of my favorites], pray
     for us
Saint Agnes, pray for us
Saint Gregory, pray for us
Saint Augustine, pray for us
Saint Athanasius, pray for us
Saint Basil, pray for us
Saint Martin, pray for us
Saint Benedict, pray for us
Saint Francis and Saint Dominic, pray for us
Saint Francis Xavier, pray for us
Saint John Vianney, pray for us
Saint Catherine, pray for us
Saint Teresa, pray for us

We reached the bottom of the page on our programs and then—the cantor kept on going! She sang through maybe twenty-five more names, rocking along, the congregation following in her wake, and I had a wild hope that maybe we could go on like this for a hundred more names at least, because by now I was almost delirious. She finally closed with "All holy men and women," and we all responded. Later, Lauren told me that Sulinda had been crying through the whole litany. It was magnificent.

The time went by; we sang, we listened, we acclaimed and said prayers. Father P.J. blessed the water, which in turn would be used to bless us. We professed our faith. We renounced the "glamour of evil," and we renounced Satan, "father of sin and prince of darkness." I liked the sound of that language: stark, literal. Not trying to accommodate both sides against the middle. Catholics still lay it on the line.

Now the initiates who hadn't been baptized at other churches approached the altar for their baptism. This was the only time when I felt a pang of envy. I'd been baptized, so I couldn't go through the rite again, but I wished I could, just for the experience. In fact, if I could have, I would have gone through full immersion. I wanted to sink into the rites, plunge in up to my ears. As it was, even the initiates being baptized could only kneel in a wading pool they had beside the baptismal font, with P.J. pouring the blessed water over their heads.

Then all the initiates gathered to profess our faith. We were almost home. We stood for the last time in the center aisle, still nervous. P.J. asked us if we believed in God, the Father almighty, creator of heaven and earth.

"We do," we said meekly, like strangled mice. P.J. cupped his ear and asked us again. We took a breath and said again, this time in a scrawny cry, "We do!"

That seemed to satisfy him. He had more questions, "Do you believe in Christ? . . . in the Holy Spirit? . . . in the one holy, Catholic and apostolic church?" Our response was better this time, more definite. It just takes some practice, I guess. Then we were asked to climb the altar steps to declare our confirmation names and be blessed once again. P.J. and Father Tom were handling this part. With Ted by my side, I went up to Father Tom. I'd chosen the confirmation name of Benedict because my path had begun at a Benedictine abbey, with Benedictine monks. Father Tom, with his big thumb, marked my forehead with the chrism, an aromatic oil smelling of balsam. A friend once told me about a church in Houston where they pour a full pint of this holy stuff, rich as honey, all over your head. That sounded wonderful, but this was good enough. I stepped down from the sanctuary, trailing a cloud of sweet perfume.

We moved through the last part of the Mass, the Liturgy of the Eucharist. This was the first time we initiates had gone through this part of the Mass since October. It felt both new and familiar as we professed the Nicene Creed, joined hands, and said the Lord's Prayer, and did all the things that real live Catholics do. Then P.J. followed the four motions of Passover and a traditional Jewish meal: take, bless, break, and offer. We all said the final words: "Lord, I am not worthy to receive you, but only say the word and I shall be healed." Then the congregation, led by the initiates, came forward to accept Holy Communion.

I'd been waiting for this moment for the past sixteen months—for all my life, without knowing it. This was the body of Christ, right here in this church, in the gathered assembly, in the hands of the priests. It seemed so simple, finally.

We moved up the aisle in two rows. I thought of paratroopers in a plane, lining up at the open door. The jump sergeant steadies them one by one, then slaps them on the back—Go!—and they step out into blue sky. I'm moving up in the left line. It looks as if I'm going to get P.J. I'm almost there. Just three more persons. Two more. One more. I can see the Host in a basket that P.J. is holding. It isn't wafers but little cubes of what look like whole-wheat bread. Somebody baked these just for Easter. How neat. How lovely.

Suddenly I'm standing in front of P.J. He takes one of the cubes, looks up, smiles at me and says, "The body of Christ."

Go!

I say firmly, "Amen." And then, finally, at last, I take the body of my Lord Jesus Christ into my mouth, and it is sweet. The taste of honey and whole wheat.

I've done it. I float over to a Eucharistic minister holding a chalice of wine and take a sip. This is the first wine, the first alcohol, I've had since I stopped drinking twelve years ago. It tastes like wine, a pleasant rosé.

I returned to the pews, pulled the kneeler out, and knelt. I was still floating, dependent but fully sustained, down into the arms of the Mother Church, and I knew that wherever I landed, yes, I would always be safe.

The Mass ended. And now everyone was standing up and hugging, and Ted gave me a big bear hug. My sister and Lauren came up. More hugs all around. We moved to the party across the courtyard. The meeting hall was all lit up, and a mariachi band was playing. Lauren was taking pictures: me and Michael, me with Sister Mary William and Skip and Scott. Michael and Barbara. Father Tom appeared in a Hawaiian shirt, genial and massive, wearing a button that said, "I Don't Remember Your Name Either."

The band played on, people were lining up for the food, and I ran around thanking everyone I could see: Michael, Barbara, Sister Mary William, the priests, the other initiates. I thanked the band. I wanted to start singing happy birthday. That was the idea, right? We went through a death and rebirth back there in the dark, right? The food was running out fast. After Mass, I was suddenly starving. I was hoping for something more substantial—you know, more Baptist. But the party was loud and happy, the band kept playing, it was the end of Lent, and with everyone, both old and new Catholics, there was a sense that we'd finally arrived at the end of a long season.

Lauren and I stayed until midnight. As we walked back through the courtyard, we passed an older couple going to the party. The man had a full white beard and was wearing a Christmas-red shirt. He noticed my name tag and pumped my hand, saying in a big gravelly voice, "Welcome to the family!"

His wife said gently, "Now dear, don't bother the boy," and he suddenly turned shy, but Lauren was delighted. Later I learned that he has thirty grandkids, so he knows about family.

When I got home, I still smelled of the chrism oil. I didn't wash it off. I wanted to go to sleep that way, with my hair and my pillow smelling of balsam.

The next morning I felt as if I'd been thrown off the back end of a truck. I moved with extreme deliberation as I made my way toward Mr. Coffeemaker. When I ran marathons, afterward, every muscle in my body would ache. My legs would ache. My back would ache. My earlobes would ache. That's how I felt now, on Easter morning.

I took Harrison, ever-patient Harrison, to 9:00 Mass. Of course, the church was packed. Hardworking Father Alan delivered the homily. He didn't use notes. After reading the Gospel, he just stepped down into the center aisle and let 'er rip. His theme was joy, everlasting joy and thanksgiving. He talked about the wonderful things in our lives, and he asked us to call out something great that had happened to us during the past year. One man said he took a bike ride with his kids, and we all applauded. A woman said that she finally became a mother this year, and we all applauded. Then I raised my hand and said, "I joined the Catholic Church last night!" and everyone applauded, and I felt brave and happy and very pleased to have my son beside me so he could hear his dad declaring out loud in front of God and everybody that, yes, he was a member of the church. And on top of that, I could take communion again! Incredible!

Back home, we had an Easter dinner with the extended family: my sister and her husband, James, and their three children, my cousin Diane with her daughter, and assorted friends of the family. It was a great meal. My brother-in-law fell asleep on the sofa. The kids played nicely. The grown-ups were able to linger at the table, having a second helping of dessert. I won't presume why, but it was the nicest Easter we'd ever spent together.

Monday morning, I slept in until 7:30, a record for me. Now it was back to telephones, deadlines, worry. People upset and under pressure. I needed a new job. But for the next four or five months, I didn't get up early or read or study or take notes or do anything Catholic at all except go to church. I felt as if a huge, bronze bell had been struck inside me, and I was simply listening as the reverberations slowly, very slowly, faded away.

Epilogue: Newly Planted

My Lord God, I have no idea where I am going.
I do not see the road ahead of me.
I cannot know for certain where it will end.
Nor do I really know myself,
and the fact that I think I am following your will
does not mean that I am actually doing so.
But I believe that the desire to please you does in fact please you.
And I hope I have that desire in all that I am doing.
I hope that I will never do anything apart from that desire.
And I know that if I do this, you will lead me by the right road,
though I may know nothing about it.
Therefore I will trust you always
though I may seem to be lost and in the shadow of death.
I will not fear, for you are ever with me,
and you will never leave me to face my perils alone.

—Thomas Merton

Christ wants us to prefer truth to him because, before being Christ, he
is truth. If you turn aside from him to go toward the truth, you will not
go far before falling into his arms.

—Simone Weil

I've spent most of my life waiting. When I was a child, I waited to grow up. When I was twelve, I wanted to just skip over adolescence altogether. I wanted to be an instant adult and not have to deal with pimples and insecurity and all the embarrassing mess of being a teenager. When I was a writer in my twenties, I waited for inspiration. I waited for my talents to mature, to have "something to say." When my father had a stroke and it was obvious that he'd never get out of bed again, I waited for him to die, and I waited as my mother grew older, thinking that somehow when both my parents were gone, I could assume their place in the family, achieve some sort of maturity, and finally "come into my own." I waited for the mail. I waited for checks. I waited for golden offers and recognition that never came. I waited a lifetime, waiting for my life to begin.

Even though I've joined the church, I can't prove that I've really gone through a conversion. Inner change is intangible. My conversion itself is something I have to take on faith. Maybe I'm just another self-involved Baby Boomer, strolling from one predictable crisis to the next, like millions of others from my generation. Some days I feel as if I'm back at the beginning, as if nothing has happened. But I can point to one thing, a change that seems definite and reassures me. I'm no longer waiting. I'm looking forward.

When I was waiting, I was always driven by a sense of entitlement. It was obvious to me that I couldn't begin living until I got what I thought I deserved. And if life didn't deliver the goods, then life wasn't being fair. But when we say that life isn't fair, we're really saying that life doesn't follow the rules we prefer. Of course life isn't fair. It's life. And God isn't "fair"—he's God, and he doesn't have to follow our rules. Even his love isn't "fair," because it's a gift freely given, not something we deserve or can earn in any way. And that's okay. That's what makes it love and not some sort of a spiritual paycheck.

Now when I'm looking forward, my sense of entitlement is slowly, very slowly being replaced by pleasant expectations. Like listening to a good story, I don't want to "get" anything; I just want to see what happens next.

On my good days—and they're not all good by any length—I see myself in a little boat moving down a river, looking ahead to discover what's around the next bend. By not waiting, I experience the present as entirely sufficient, and the future is gravy, a bonus that goes on and on. It's only when I drift away from God's love that I have those old feelings of awful termination. Most of us have to come to an end before we can begin again.

And I keep on beginning. Part of conversion is accepting that it never stops. I think of a Tibetan prayer wheel spinning around with its little drum stuffed with prayers. We never stop turning. I like to think of heaven as eternal grad school: always converting, always learning more, forever. I'm not talking about knowing a bunch of stuff but the process itself, the experience of understanding, the aha! moment when the puzzle comes together. God will be our teacher, of course, the best in the universe, and the lessons have already begun here on earth.

When I was waiting, I thought I knew my proper destination. In my twenties I even outlined my entire career: how many books written by what age, how many awards, how far my reputation extended by the age of forty, fifty, and so on. None of this happened, and that's probably a gift. Otherwise, I might have been deluded by success into thinking I was the proprietor of my destiny—captain of my ship, master of my soul, and all that other silliness about absolute self-determinism.

Now I only know that I won't be alone with my future. In fact, I realize that my future is less about me than it is about God, about other people, about everything in the universe. It's about how I love and express this love, not who I am or what I've been given. In the final and truest sense, I'm not the point of my own story, and my story doesn't end with me.

Maybe I'm reading too much into my little life. But what would I be missing if I didn't try to understand everything around me as a running translation of this infinite love? The signs are everywhere. I've spent most of my life arriving at the obvious, so I'm still learning that the way to heaven is through the world—not beyond it or above it but straight through all the webbing and snarl of daily life, and straight through the happiness as well that God places on our doorstep every day.

So I'll keep looking forward, though I don't know where I'm going, only how. I'll try to recognize along the way the gifts I've been given and, more important, that I can pass these gifts along to others. When I started the RCIA process, I asked my parish to lead me along. Now I would hope to help lead others.

As Carmen would say, God is crazy about all of us, without exception, and as we accept this love, all at once or by slow degrees, we can always have something amazing to share, something heart-wrenching, loving, honest and wild, something sweet and burning, like a gift of fire. We can all have wonderful news.

Thanks

A wholly inadequate bouquet of thanks to the Benedictine community at Corpus Christi Abbey and Carmen Zabalégui; to Michael Flahive, Ted and Carole Hatfield, Joe and Sue Webber, and all the RCIA team members at St. Austin; to Fathers Patrick Johnson, Tom Foley, Alan Oakes, and Rick Wilkinson; to St. Austin's Small Christian Community of Contemplative Prayer; to Joe Durepos and his colleagues at Loyola Press; and especially to Lauren and our boys, Harrison and Spencer, for their understanding and patience with this particular convert.

Resources

One of the great advantages of Catholicism is that it has a very, very long bookshelf. The list below includes some of the books I read while going through the RCIA, as well as others I've found since then. I've also included a sample of excellent films that speak to me as a Catholic.

Books

Autobiography by St. Teresa of Ávila. Anything by this great saint is worth reading. An amazing marriage of the sublime and the down-to-earth.

Father Joe: The Man Who Saved My Soul by Tony Hendra. Conversations with a monk who is filled with wisdom, humor, and God's own love.

Five Great Catholic Ideas by Father Edward Clark. An excellent synopsis. Helps explain what it means to "think like a Catholic."

Gilead and *Home* by Marilynne Robinson. The author, who happens to be a Calvinist, writes novels that are dazzling in their ability to present characters who live fully and naturally in their Christian faith.

God, I Have Issues: 50 Ways to Pray No Matter How You Feel by Mark Thibodeaux. A practical guide to praying when we really don't feel prayerful.

Morality: The Catholic View by Servais Pinckaers. A positive approach to morality based not on lists of obligations and prohibitions but on the classic idea that virtue leads to a happy life.

Mother Theresa: Come Be My Light. Her private writings that show a soul who never lost faith but endured a dark night of the soul for decades.

My Life with the Saints by James Martin. An autobiography that describes his life as a Jesuit. A most entertaining author. See also his *Jesuit Guide to (Almost) Everything, This Our Exile, In Good Company*, and *Between Heaven and Mirth*.

Open Mind, Open Heart by Father Thomas Keating. A Trappist monk, Keating has written this and many other books to explain to modern readers the centuries-long tradition of contemplative prayer.

Story of a Soul: The Autobiography of St. Thérèse of Lisieux. One of my favorite saints. *The Little Way of Saint Thérèse of Lisieux: Into the Arms of Love* by John Nelson is a brief but well-chosen anthology of her writings.

The Cloister Walk and *Amazing Grace* by Kathleen Norris. Describes her conversion, the monastic life, problems of modern doubt, prayer, idolatry, and other topics related to faith.

The Cloud of Unknowing, author unknown. A masterpiece of medieval mysticism.

The Essence of Prayer by Ruth Burrows. One of the best books I've seen on this subject. Very austere but profound. I'd also recommend her *Guidelines to Mystical Prayer*.

The Imitation of Christ by Thomas à Kempis. One of those books I'd want on a desert island. Read this book; it will make you strong.

The Prodigal Son by Henri Nouwen. Anything by this teacher and priest is worth reading. Go to him if you're looking for a definition of Christian love.

The Rule of St. Benedict by St. Benedict. Written in the sixth century for monastic communities, this short book of precepts has been used by many other communities and individuals as a guide for living a Christian life. Wise, practical, and balanced.

The Sanctifier by Archbishop Luis Martinez. Talks about the Holy Spirit in the context of the Trinity, how we can move by the Holy Spirit to the Son to the Father. A wonderful book with a truly poetic vision of God.

The Seven Storey Mountain by Thomas Merton, a Trappist monk. One of the most popular conversion stories of our time. See also *New Seeds of Contemplation, No Man Is an Island, Conjectures of a Guilty Bystander*, and many other books by this prolific author.

Thomas Aquinas, Theologian by Thomas O'Meara, a Franciscan priest. Absolutely stunning. Presents Aquinas as someone who used the scholastic philosophy more as a "scaffolding" for what was essentially a mystical understanding of God, humanity, and the universe.

Traveling Mercies by Anne Lamott. A funny, candid, and contemporary conversion story, both reverent and irreverent.

Twilight of Atheism by Alister McGrath. He argues that the Enlightenment has really been only a kind of odd, often bloody, detour that came to an end symbolically with the fall of the Berlin Wall.

Waiting for God by Simone Weil. A collection of writings by a brilliant twentieth-century philosopher who was never confirmed as a Catholic but spent her life on the threshold of the church.

What Happens at Mass by Jeremy Driscoll, a Benedictine priest. The best little book I've read on the Mass.

Film

Babette's Feast. More than about food, this film is a celebration of God's creation. Voted a top film by the Vatican.

Catholicism: Journey to the Heart of the Faith. Written and produced by Father Robert Barron, this is an intelligent yet very accessible introduction. See also his organization's website, wordonfire.org.

Groundhog Day. Bill Murray in a modern story of change and redemption. I checked it out when I heard it was popular with the Jesuits.

Into Great Silence. A beautiful film covering several winter months in a Carthusian monastery in France. Very little dialogue, as is appropriate in a contemplative order.

Of Gods and Men. Absolutely wonderful and very moving. An intelligent film about the ultimate choices we can make for God.

Romero. The life of Archbishop Óscar Romero, who opposed, at great personal risk, the anti-Catholic political forces in El Salvador.

The Mission. Robert De Niro and Jeremy Irons in a story—sometimes violent—about Jesuit missionary work in eighteenth-century South America.

Thérèse (directed by Alain Cavalier). Most films about St. Thérèse are sweet but a bit sappy. This one is an elegant, spare, and beautiful work.

About the Author

Richard Cole is the author of two collections of poetry: *The Glass Children* (The University of Georgia Press) and *Success Stories* (Limestone Books). His poetry and prose have been published in the *New Yorker*, *Poetry*, *The Sun*, *Hudson Review*, and *Image Journal: Good Letters*. He works as a business writer in Austin, Texas. Visit www.richard-cole.net to learn more.

Continue the Conversation

If you enjoyed this book, then connect with Loyola Press to continue the conversation, engage with other readers, and find out about new and upcoming books from your favorite spiritual writers.

Visit us at **LoyolaPress.com** to create an account and register for our newsletters.

Or scan the code on the left with your smartphone.

Connect with us through:

 Facebook
facebook.com
/loyolapress

 Twitter
twitter.com
/loyolapress

 YouTube
youtube.com
/loyolapress

Also Available

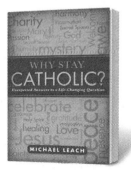

Why Stay Catholic?
Unexpected Answers to a
Life-Changing Question

MICHAEL LEACH
$14.95 • Paperback • 3537-5

Rock-Bottom Blessings
Discovering God's Abundance
When All Seems Lost

KAREN BEATTIE
$13.95 • Paperback • 3842-0

The Thorny Grace of It
And Other Essays for
Imperfect Catholics

BRIAN DOYLE
$14.95 • Paperback • 3906-9

To order: call 800-621-1008,
visit www.loyolapress.com/store,
or visit your local bookseller.